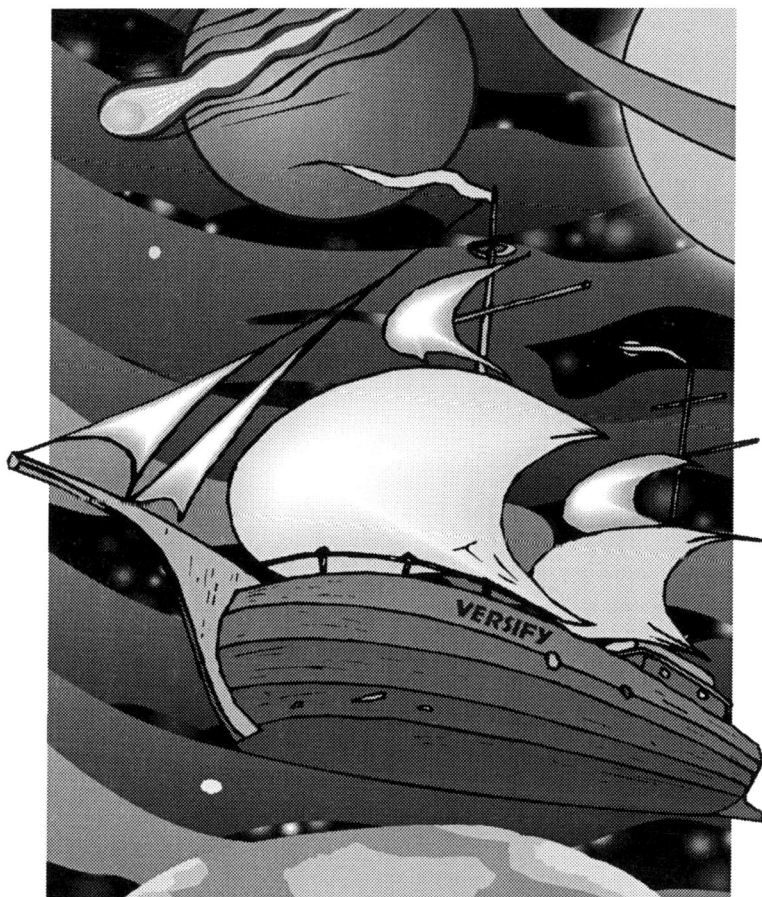

POETIC VOYAGES
EAST LANCASHIRE

Edited by Steve Twelvetree

First published in Great Britain in 2001 by
YOUNG WRITERS
Remus House,
Coltsfoot Drive,
Peterborough, PE2 9JX
Telephone (01733) 890066

Copyright Contributors 2001

HB ISBN 0 75433 380 9
SB ISBN 0 75433 381 7

FOREWORD

Young Writers was established in 1991 with the aim to promote creative writing in children, to make reading and writing poetry fun.

This year once again, proved to be a tremendous success with over 88,000 entries received nationwide.

The Poetic Voyages competition has shown us the high standard of work and effort that children are capable of today. It is a reflection of the teaching skills in schools, the enthusiasm and creativity they have injected into their pupils shines clearly within this anthology.

The task of selecting poems was therefore a difficult one but nevertheless, an enjoyable experience. We hope you are as pleased with the final selection in *Poetic Voyages East Lancashire* as we are.

CONTENTS

St Michael & All Angels CE Primary School, Colne

Kim Fish	79
Bethany Dyson	80
Josh Titley	80
Chelsea Singleton	80
Laura Widdup	81
Elizabeth Cox	82
Jak Carradice	82
Emily Jayne Lee	83
Kyle Wimbles	83
Charlotte Percival	83
Cory Howarth	84
Layla Birtwistle	84
Craig Wiseman	85
Luke Hardy	85
Ruth French	85
Alexander Shorrock	86
Emily Birtwell	86
Amy Monaghan	87

St Peter's CE Primary School, Accrington

Dionne Ashworth Howorth	87
Shaista Hussain	88
Bronwyn Stirzaker	89
Emma Archer	89
Lauren Beaumont	90
Ricky Gudgeon	90
Soaib Khan	91
Laura Whittaker	91
Jacob Sledden	92
Saria Akhtar	92
Lita Lord	93

St Veronica's RC Primary School, Rossendale

Matthew Allen	94
Laura Starkie	94
Daniel Nightingale	95
Laura-Jane Hindle	95

Romy Beagan	96
Aaron Morris	96
Charlotte Harling	97
Clare Burrows	97
Gerard Manley	98
Julianna Brougham	98
Jenna Chattwood	99
Katherine Parry	100
Jenny Conroy	100
Edward Ainsworth	101
Chelsea Frost	102
Robyn Kay	102
Laura O'Gara	103
Aimee Hilton	103
Charles McIntyre	104
Elizabeth Ainsworth	104
Daniel Gibirdi	105
Catherine Haworth	106
Adam Cook	106
Rebecca Slinger	107
William Eaton	108
Lauren Mason	109
William Mason	110
Natasha Stanley	111
Conor McGirr	112
Hannah Valentine	112
Joe Nangle	113
Hannah Connolly	114
Niamh Baxendale	114
Thomas Walmsley	115

Shade Junior & Infant School

Kristian Garland	116
Patrick Ramsbottom	117
Alex Hill	117
Elizabeth Uttley	118
Ashli Cullen	119
Tamsin Connor	120

The Poems

Vampires About

Vampires are nasty evil things
Chaos is the thing it brings
He'll drain the blood from your body
Your skin'll wither and go all soggy
He cannot stand the light of day
But in a fight he'll keep you at bay
Sometimes he says I really must fly
I've got some people to suck dry
I'm awfully tired I must sleep
Today I killed a few sheep.
Some people opened my coffin lid
Where inside I was hid
The stake went into my heart and stuck out my back
Safety is what I lack.

Marc Perkins (11)
Barrow VC Primary School

Monsters

I was in my garden
On my swing
Then I saw a weird looking thing!
I ran inside
Where's my mum?
Then cried and sucked my thumb!
I ran upstairs, is she there?
No! But I see my dad's underwear!

Martha Lassey (10)
Barrow VC Primary School

FISHES

Fishes in the sea,
Fishes in your tea.
Fishes, fishes thick as a plank,
Fishes, fishes in your tank.
Fishes, fishes that's the end of the fishes' story,
Fishes, fishes oh how boring.

Oliver Grindley (10)
Barrow VC Primary School

THE TEACHER

Poor old teacher, we missed you so,
When in hospital you had to go,
For you to remain there is a sin,
We're sorry about the banana skin!

Danielle Brooks (11)
Barrow VC Primary School

SCHOOL

He laughed when they said it couldn't be done
He smiled and said he knew it
But he tried the thing that couldn't be done
And found he couldn't do it.

Farrah Burns (10)
Barrow VC Primary School

2

AWAY

Away at camp
Away at sea
I wonder which place I could be?

Away at camp we play games,
Away at sea my fears go away.

Away at camp
Away at sea
I wonder which place I could be?

Sarah Chew (10)
Barrow VC Primary School

TREES

The tree outside has started to grow
Its branches are crispy brown
My dad's going to cut it down
But I put a banana skin on the floor
And now he's lying on the ground!

Laura Simpson (11)
Barrow VC Primary School

CATERPILLARS

Trees, trees are so bright
When stars shine at night
Copse, grove all sorts of trees!
With shining, tasty, green, green leaves.

Gary Micallef (11)
Barrow VC Primary School

MOUNTAIN RISE

The sun peeps over the peak of a mountain
It's now the start of the morn
The animals awaken from their sleep
To see that it is dawn
After the farmer has finished yawning
He looks up in the sky
While in his house his wife is baking
A nice hot shepherd's pie
The sun keeps rising higher, higher
As the day goes on
Because the sun has just arisen
It's a long time 'fore it's gone.

Joshua Miller (10)
Barrow VC Primary School

ODE TO A BUS STOP

Oh you marvellous bus stop
As I stand there drowning in the rain
Oh how I wish you had a shelter
To cover me from the rain
But I would never complain
I have longed to say that you will see the day
That you will have to stand in the rain
So don't you complain.
One day the council put up a shelter
After that day it never rained.

Claire Holgate (11)
Barrow VC Primary School

DAYDREAM

Tiger attacking
Attention lacking
Invasion of the fleas,
Books out please
Pirates coming ashore,
Sums more, more, more
Winning the Olympics
Teacher giving pupils ticks
Then I snap out of my daydream
What will teacher say
When she sees how little work I've done today?

Jessica Houghton (10)
Barrow VC Primary School

CHOCOLATE

Brown, white, cream and . . .
Oh! I love chocolate!
Nice and creamy,
Soft and dreamy,
My tummy screaming
'Feed me, feed me!'
I've nearly finished all my tea
I'll grab the chocolate and then I'll flee
Nice and creamy,
Soft and dreamy,
My tummy screaming
'Feed me, feed me!'

Helen Duxbury (11)
Barrow VC Primary School

I Am

I'm the racing horse,
I'm the green of grass,
I'm the cuddly teddy bear,
I'm the shimmering glass.

I'm the thunder and lightning,
I'm the cheetah flash,
I'm the big roller coaster,
I'm the sea's splash.

I'm the diving dolphin,
I'm the Olympic game,
I'm the winner in everything,
I'm a rich person with lots of fame.

I'm as sweet as sugar,
I'm the fizzy Coke,
I'm the golden eagle,
I'm the Titanic boat.

I'm the wool on the sheep,
Still I'm not Little Bo Peep,
I'm the best in the crew,
I'm the tiger in the zoo.

I'm the first morning gasp,
I'm the orange in the flask,
I'm the best of the lot,
I'm the baby in the cot.

I'm the sun shining through,
I'm the cow that likes to chew,
I'm the music on the Top Of The Pops,
I'm the dog's jazzy spots.

This is what I am
But most of all I'm me!

Heather Whalley (10)
Brennand's Endowed Primary School

TRACTORS

T   ractors are large with big
R   ound wheels,
A   nd a big bonnet, the exhaust
C   oughs up smoke,
T   ractors all together are good,
O   range ones I don't like except for
R   enaults they are
S   uperb.

Peter Handley (10)
Brennand's Endowed Primary School

THE DOGS

I like dogs and they like me
Because I feed them nicely.

Not all dogs can be kind to people
Because they don't know people.

Beatrice Redfearn (8)
Brennand's Endowed Primary School

THE SWAN

The swan a graceful and elegant creature,
So tender and gentle,
Its feathers gleam like frost,
Its beak is like lightning
It glides through the water gracefully,
Its eyes are as black as coal.

It puts its head in the water scanning for food,
Its eggs are a creamy blue,
Then crack! The egg opens and a baby swan comes waddling out,
Widdle, waddle, widdle, waddle
It walks with its graceful mother.

Kimberley Tedstone (10)
Brennand's Endowed Primary School

WATER

It washes, it whooshes, it splashes, it slushes,
It girgles, it mirgles, it pirgles, it slirgles,
It flows, it's wet, it gushes, it waves,
It's gentle, it's quite, it's slow, it's graceful,
It's noisy, it's hard, it's fierce, it's swift,
It whirls, it hurls, it curls, it twirls,
It's blue, it's green, it's muddy, it's clear,
I need it, you need it, everyone does,
It bubbles, it boils, it twists, it evaporates,
What is it?
Water.

Richard Ankers (10)
Brennand's Endowed Primary School

I'm Going On Safari

I'm going on safari,
The sun is shining bright.
I'm going out bat hunting,
In the middle of the night.

The sun is shining bright,
We're going to see a giraffe.
We're going to see a hippo
And a hyena and its laugh.

We're going to see a giraffe,
Going down to the lagoon.
We're going to see it drinking,
In the pale light of the moon.

Down at the lagoon,
I'm going to meet Kinari.
He will be our tour guide,
I'm going on safari.

Caroline Russell-Smith (11)
Brennand's Endowed Primary School

Cars Are . . .

C   ars are the best
A   ctive and speedy,
R   acing round the rally course
S   uch great machines.

A   great machine,
R   allying is the best
E   ngines roar when you give them full throttle.

Thomas Barlow (11)
Brennand's Endowed Primary School

WHEN FLYING

When flying in the air,
You can go anywhere,
You twist and twirl,
Then you hurl.

When flying in the air,
You admire the white polar bears,
Also the running brown hares,
When flying in the air.

When flying in the air,
You see golden eagles,
Swoop down to see the beetles,
When flying in the air.

When flying in the air,
You admire the view,
When flying in the air,
You can go anywhere!

James Gott (10)
Brennand's Endowed Primary School

WHO AM I?

A scary creature,
A hiding creature,
A fast creature,
A spotty creature,
Put it together, what have you got?
A leopard.

An African creature,
An enormous creature,
A blue creature,
Put it together, what have you got?
A big elephant.

A woolly creature,
A noisy creature,
A farming creature,
A baby creature,
Put it together, what have you got?
A lamb.

Daniel Parker (8)
Brennand's Endowed Primary School

IN THE WILD

In the wild it's very scary
I saw a monkey that went crazy
Then I met a cow that went 'moo'
In the very low voice so I said 'shoo'
Then I went to the hippopotamus hunt
I nearly stood on one
And it nearly bit my bum!
Then something very scary
Guess what?
I am not going to tell you!

Emma Turner (8)
Brennand's Endowed Primary Schoo

CALVING

C   alves need to be fed,
A   ll different breeds,
L   ots and lots of calves,
V   ery nice indeed,
I   t takes a lot to fill them,
N   ever are they full,
G   oing home at the end of the day is nice.

Thomas Harrison (10)
Brennand's Endowed Primary School

THE BEE

I know a bee,
Who likes drinking tea.

Then one day
She went out to play,
But she didn't share with friend Bea
Because she had such excellent tea.

I know a bee,
Who likes drinking tea.

Once she was ill
And had to take a pill,
'Now' said Doctor Bee
'It's time to drink some tea'.

I know a bee,
Who likes drinking tea.

Marianne Russell-Smith (8)
Brennand's Endowed Primary School

REMEMBER, REMEMBER THE FIFTH OF NOVEMBER

Remember, remember the fifth of November
When it goes spooky and dark
All the fireworks start,
The bang in the
Sky makes you feel warm inside,
Then you see the Catherine wheel
Go round and round,
And that makes and sparks fly to the ground,
It is such a good day,
So you'll always remember the fifth of November.

Timmy Ankers (8)
Brennand's Endowed Primary School

MY FRIENDS

I have a friend called Het
She wants to be a vet.
I have a friend called Maz
Her sister is called Caz, they like doing jazz.
There is Bee
She likes being free.
There is Kate
She eats her food on a plate.
There is Rach
She likes the letter H.
That is all of my friends.

Victoria Rowland (8)
Brennand's Endowed Primary School

THE SNOW POEM

Snow falls in the winter
Winter is very bitter
Snow is cool
Like a big iced up pool.

The snow got in my shoes
And socks
But who cares, snow is tops
Some snow is slushy
I woke up and my hair was all bushy.

When the snow started to end
I watched it with a friend
I watched the snow disappear
I can't wait until next year.

Daniel McKenzie (9)
Chatburn CE Primary School

SNOWY GAMES

Snow is falling very fast,
Want to go sledging,
Hope it will last.

Hat and coat, wellies too,
Wrap up warm,
There's lots to do.

Snow is drifting against the wall,
Make us a snowman,
Make it tall.

Snowball fights with my friend,
I hope it won't go,
I hope it won't end.

Snow is going, what a shame,
Turn into slush,
And down the drain.

Eleanor Singleton (9)
Chatburn CE Primary School

SNOW

Chilly winter brings the snow
Icy winds begin to blow
Fragile snowflakes rush around
Settle softly on the ground.

It lays like a carpet soft and still
A family comes sledging over the hill
A good time is had by one and all
But still more silver snowflakes fall.

A new day dawns and brings the sun
The vast white carpet starts to run
Snowflakes cry as they disappear
They run away like a tear
Slowly, slowly they fade away.

An empty patch where they used to lay.

Rebecca Stratton (11)
Chatburn CE Primary School

SNOW POEM

The snow, the snow makes the wind blow.

The snow makes my nose glow.

When you build a snowman
In the snow the sun will melt it
And make it go.

When you go out in the snow you
Get wetter but when you're inside
You get much better.

I chucked a snowball in my mate's face
Her glasses fell off and broke her brace.

I went on a sledge and I accidentally flew into a hedge.

I had a snowball fight with my mates
And one snowball hit somebody's gate.

I had a snowball fight with my dad
One hit my neck and hurt really bad.

I rode a motorbike in the snow
The back wheel got stuck and wouldn't go.

Karen Hanson (10)
Chatburn CE Primary School

SCHOOL RULES

Don't draw on tables.
Look at your times tables.
Don't swear.
Share!
Don't wear party clothes.
School uniform we loathe.
Don't call names.
Let them join in your games.
Don't be naughty.
Think thoughtfully.
Mind your own business,
Or no Christmas.
Don't run,
Or you will get done.
Keep, keep, keep, keep, keep your
Rules!

Rebekah Gorman (9) & Louise Paul (8)
Chatburn CE Primary School

HEAD TEACHERS

The head teacher is helpful and delightful.
He gives us funny looks when he reads lots of books.
He tripped up on the carpet and blew a gasket.
He got into a mood and put us all in solitude.
Shouted at us all, we were scared.
He was very savage and he did a lot of damage
Our head teacher.

Merissa Whitaker & Joanna Kennerley (8)
Chatburn CE Primary School

IT'S A SNOWY DAY

Winnie the Pooh goes in the snow,
The holly is dropping from my door.

I made a snowman the other day,
Faye my friend came to stay.

The snow is white like my lamp,
Snowflakes are a bit damp.

Icicles turn into ice,
Snow is crispy and very nice.

In the winter it's all cold and white,
We all join in, in snowball fights.

We all like going sledging with our friends,
In the snow we make dens.

Molly Gladwin (10)
Chatburn CE Primary School

SNOW

Snow, snow, snow
Falling from the sky,
All the little birds,
Are flying very high,
Children laughing, shouting with glee,
Because they can slide happily
Branches of trees are heavy and full,
They look picturesque
Graceful and tall,
An illusion of beauty,
Beholden to all.

Claire Reynolds (9)
Chatburn CE Primary School

INFANTS

Infants are sticky, good and picky,
Infants are trying, hot and crying,
Infants are muddy, boiling and hungry,
Infants aren't strong or wrong,
Infants have mice and like spice,
Infants run! It's Miss Nice.

Infants are cute,
Nice lice ah!
Sorry for the interruption
Wow! Volcano eruption,
Sorry for the sudden earthquake,
Oh no! Lava all over our cake!
Infants run! The bossy teacher is coming,
Now they're hiding behind a bush,
What's that noise? She's coming, *shush!*

Infants are cool,
Infants stand on a stool,
Infants are smelly,
Infants watch the telly,
Infants are cheerful,
Infants are tearful,
Infants always want attention,
Infants always avoid detention,
Infants shout so loud,
Sorry for the sudden sound.

Infants are small and tall,
Infants are playful and loveable,
Infants are always in my way,
Infants always want to play.
Infants! Infants! Infants!

Phoebe Williams & Charlotte Smith (8)
Rebecca Wilson & Amanda Smalley (9)
Chatburn CE Primary School

SNOW

It's snowing, get up quick,
Brush your teeth and clean the sink,
Get dressed as fast as you can,
We'll go out and build a snowman.

Put all the snow in the wheelbarrow,
Don't push it too fast, watch the sparrow,
Pile all the snow on the ground,
The neighbours are still in bed, don't make a sound.

A carrot for his nose,
And then I suppose
Some buttons for his chest,
Now he really is the best.

Amy Moorhouse (10)
Chatburn CE Primary School

SNOW, SNOW

Snow, snow go away, that's what my mum always says!
Matthew and me shout with glee
Whenever the snow lays under the tree.
We come down the hill on our sledge
Daddy even went under the hedge.
It's wet and cold, but oh such fun
My fingers get cold and very numb
Oh how sad, when the snow turns to rain
We grab our sledge
And go home again
When I get home I'm ready for tea,
And I hope that mum has a bath ready for me!

Lillie Dugdale (9)
Chatburn CE Primary School

SCHOOL RULES

Be kind to others,
And not your brothers.

Don't be silly in class,
And don't break any glass.

Don't run in school,
Or else you'll be a fool.

Fix up a board,
And you'll get a head teacher's award!

Don't throw your fork,
Or else you'll be a dork.

Don't stare into space,
Or else you'll get a pie in your face.

Don't poo in your pants
Else you'll turn into ants.

Don't spit at teachers
Else they'll turn into creatures.

Don't draw on the table
Or you'll get a label.

Tom Stratton, Richard Park, Iain Metcalfe,
Jordan Marsden & Callum Heanan (8)
Lauren Crook (9)
Chatburn CE Primary School

SNOW DAYS

Snow is soft, snow is cold,
It makes your fingers tingle,
Wrap up warm we're always told,
In the breeze the icicles jingle.

Snowy days are white,
And sledging I like to go,
The snow is so bright,
And snowballs I like to throw.

Snowmen we like to make,
With a big orange carrot for his nose,
It reminds me of a Christmas cake,
And by the fire we warm our toes.

Daniel Buckle (10)
Chatburn CE Primary School

SNOW WHITE DAY

S   now comes cold,
N   ight or day,
O   nly in,
W   intertime.

W   hite tops on
H   ills bright,
I   n caps of white,
T   he snow scene,
E   xciting the eye.

D   oing its best,
A   t this time of
Y   ear to bring some cheer.

Becky Petty-Jones (11)
Chatburn CE Primary School

SNOW

Silently falling onto the land
Covering grass and hills all around
Cold and crisp, a blanket of white,
Oh what a beautiful sight.

Snowflakes all different
Fall from the sky
Onto the children
As they pass by.

Excited children filled with glee
Stand in wonder at all they see
Snowmen and snowball, cold fingers and toes
When will it come again.
Nobody knows!

Amy Rignall (10)
Chatburn CE Primary School

SNOW

Snow is white
It is good for a snowball fight.
Snow is skiddy
It makes me giddy.
Snow is slushy,
Snow is mushy,
I can build a snowman
Or I can throw it as far as I can.
When the snow falls from the sky
I have a mince pie.
Snow is lots of fun
I can make skiddy patches with my bum.

Craig Wood (10)
Chatburn CE Primary School

HEAD TEACHERS

They give certificates for good work
They say they don't but they all drive a Merc.

Sometimes he is very scary,
Sometimes he makes me wary.

He is always trying
But never crying.

He used to live in a city,
He's not got a lot of pity.

He has a very big pen,
In fact he's got about ten.

The head teachers,
They are creatures.

Sarah Haworth & Kimberly Harrison (8)
Chatburn CE Primary School

MY FAVOURITE TEACHER

My favourite teacher is Mrs Bushbey
Remember she's always nice.
She teaches all my favourite lessons
But she teaches some I don't like.
Usually she teaches her own class
She is the teacher of 6B.
Her hair is short, brown and curly
But she always wears it down.
Everybody likes her
You will too when you see her.

Jade Chadburn (7)
Lowerhouse Junior School

THE WORST CLASS IN THE SCHOOL

Alex is throwing pencils across the room.
Louis is hitting Adam with the broom.
Ashley is on the floor.
Alexander's banging on the door.
Eric is jumping on the tables.
Jordan's ripping up the book of fables.
Jonathan is writing on the board.
Jack thinks he is the lord.
Sean is throwing a tantrum.
Lee thinks he is a phantom.
Daniel's banging his head on the wall.
Paul is running in the hall.
Mrs Davey said 'We're going on a trip now'
All the class said 'Wow!'
Arron said 'How?'
Billy was in a rush
Joely kissed him, it made him blush.

Joe Barraclough (10)
Lowerhouse Junior School

MY PETS

I have one cat,
I have one mouse,
I have them running round my house.
I have two hamsters,
I wanted snakes,
All these pets are big mistakes.

Emma Steele (9)
Lowerhouse Junior School

FOOTBALL

Saturday comes, match day is here,
Me and my dad go for a beer,
I have a pie and a bottle of coke
Then on to the match with a laugh and a joke,
With my scarf and my shirt
The teams come out
So smart and alert.
The ref blows his whistle for the game to start
It reminds me of when I played in the park.
Bags for goalposts, my sister in goal,
I scored a goal just like Andy Cole.
We won four - nil
I was man of the match,
Time to go home I've a bus to catch,
My tea will be ready waiting for me to eat,
I wish it was Saturday every day of the week.

Louis Hobson (10)
Lowerhouse Junior School

MY BUNNY

My bunny last made me laugh
When I said to him have a bath.
In the morning bunny's there
Waiting for me to brush his hair.
His feet are where he has to eat
My bunny likes to run
And have a bit of fun
When I go to feed it
He has made a pit.

Stephanie Kime (10)
Lowerhouse Junior School

MY PETS

My rabbits eat and drink all day
At night they snuggle up in hay
I feed and water them
And they eat and drink it again.

My cat chases mice
And that is not nice
I stroke her cute head
When she is in her bed.

My dog always barks like every dog does
And he is not very intelligent like us
He thinks he can
Chase the postman.

Lauren Marlor (10)
Lowerhouse Junior School

I'VE DREAMED

I've always dreamed of being an astronaut,
A police officer too,
Or maybe a teacher,
Or working in a zoo!
I might be a make-up artist
I dreamed that I could work
In a football team.
I'd love to be a cook too!
I wish I could decide just what to do!

Lindsey Zirins (10)
Lowerhouse Junior School

THE NAUGHTY BOY

One day I saw a naughty boy
Who came and attacked me with his toy.
He decided to aim straight for my head
And jumped on my back like I was a bed.
So then I said 'You naughty boy
How dare you hit me with a toy'.
But the boy just laughed and then he said,
'This is a very comfy bed'.
Then came along his lovely mum,
She smacked him on his little bum,
The boy just screamed but also said
'You were a very comfy bed'.

Jamie Robinson (10)
Lowerhouse Junior School

FOOTBALL FEVER

When it comes to Saturday
I go to watch Burnley play
I set off to go at quarter-past one
And hope that Burnley win
But if they are playing away
I can't go and watch Burnley play
When it comes to a Saturday
I go to watch Burnley play
I get some Coke and some sweets and
Say to my dad Burnley will win
And if they don't I will scream
Scream, scream!

Adam Merrifield (10)
Lowerhouse Junior School

TABITHA

My cat is called Tabby
For the colour of her fur
When I stroke her she'll purr and purr
Her favourite place is on my knee
She'll stay there all day content with me
But when it's time for her to play
She has a tartan mouse to chase away
Up into the air it goes
Then she catches it with her paws.

Claire Scott (9)
Lowerhouse Junior School

SCHOOL

As I was walking down the street
All my friends I did meet
We're on our way to school
Oops! I fell, what a silly fool
School has finished it's three o'clock
Just got home, dog ate my sock.

Samantha Cousins (9)
Lowerhouse Junior School

GA, GA, GA, GA, GOO, GOO

Dipping fingers in the custard
Ga, ga, ga, ga, goo, goo.

Taking his nappy off when he shouldn't do
Ga, ga, ga, ga, goo, goo.

Hitting people's heads
Ga, ga, ga, ga, goo, goo.

And he's a baby.
Ga, ga, ga, ga, goo, goo.

Alex-Ray Harvey (10)
Lowerhouse Junior School

TREES

Trees are good,
Trees aren't bad,
Trees are happy,
Trees aren't sad,
Trees are friendly,
Trees aren't mad,
Trees are the best thing
Man could ever have.

Rebecca Stanworth (9)
Lowerhouse Junior School

TREES

Trees are green,
Trees are brown,
Trees are here,
And all around.
Some are short,
Some are tall,
Conker trees can
Be quite fun.

Lauren Pilkington (9)
Lowerhouse Junior School

THE ZOO

The monkeys go bang and the cows go crazy,
The lions roar and elephants are so noisy,
The bulls all charge, and the ducks go quack, quack
The dogs all chase the cats
And frogs all dive in the water,
And crocodiles all go snap, snap,
Hens go cluck, cluck
And parrots copy what you say,
And birds go peck, peck,
And lizards change colour.

Katie Hargreaves (8)
Lowerhouse Junior School

MY CAT IS FAT

I have a cat
He is fat
Every day he sits on the mat.
He licks his paws
And hides in the draws
And scratches his paws
On the old drawers.

Daniel Mowbray (11)
Lowerhouse Junior School

MY BROTHER'S FERRETS

Some people think ferrets are scary
Not like dogs and cats
But my brother thinks they're ace
He even gives them a bath.

He plays with them till bedtime
But you'll be happy to know
He doesn't take them to bed
They sleep in the shed.

Melissa Haworth (9)
Lowerhouse Junior School

NIGHT

Not much sound in the night
You can't see very much light
You can hear some funny sounds
Like the howl of howling hounds
The flicker of lights from passing cars
I can see the outline of shiny stars
Going to sleep in the night
Drifting off without any fright
Going, going, going, gone, zzzzz.

Jamie Ryding (9)
Lowerhouse Junior School

THINGS I HEAR AT NIGHT

I hear voices in the night
Everything is out of sight.
I hear the sound of the telly
And a rumble of my belly.
I can hear the ring of the phone
And the sound of a car horn.
I can hear my dad making the tea
And the sound of a buzzing bee.

Sarah Ridgway (9)
Lowerhouse Junior School

RED ROSE

Red Rose you are beautiful
Red Rose your scent is lovely,
But you have thorns
Which are very sharp,
And may hurt somebody.

Lilac Lily how beautiful you are,
Making me really happy,
But you grow too quickly
And the flower bed might get too crowded,
Like too many people in a car.

Betty Bluebell as blue as the sky,
You make me happy,
You never make me cry
But soon you will die,
Never to be seen again.

Holly Hyacinth as white as snow,
You seem to survive in winds that blow,
But you seem so still,
Never on the go.

So all flowers are beautiful,
But some have their ups and downs,
They make happy smiles,
Never bad frowns.

Lucy Zirins (8)
Lowerhouse Junior School

MY PONY

Over the fields and far away
My pony and I go out to play.
Elsa's a piebald, nearly six
She's full of fun and rarely kicks.

She tosses her head and flicks her tail,
And eats her oats from a yellow pail
She and I are such very good friends,
I hope this friendship never ends.

I love her and she loves me
And we are one in harmony.
Over the fields and far away
My pony and I go out to play.

Charlotte Jaggers (9)
Lowerhouse Junior School

THE DRAGON FOOTBALLER

The dragon joined the football team
He kicked the ball and scored a goal
The dragon that joined the football team.

He ran and ran and crushed a football fan
And then he took the ball and scored a goal
The dragon who crushed a football fan.

He fell, ran and ate a man
Took the ball and scored a goal
The dragon who ate a man
The dragon that joined the football team.

Eric Jones (10)
Lowerhouse Junior School

Invite To All Children

Take one end of my ball of lace
You're invited to an amazing place.

Just follow my enchanted lace,
And you'll be in my special place.

Loopy loop around the trees,
No bugs, no flies, just honey bees.

There's something hidden in the trees,
It's not just nests of bumble bees.

Now you've met my special friend,
At last your journey's at an end.

Roxanne Barker (10)
Lowerhouse Junior School

The Golden Sea

I dreamed a dream that I could fly
And that I saw a great big pie
Flying high above my head,
Flashing blue and green and red.
One of these doors in front of me,
Must lead to the golden sea.
I open one look over there,
The golden sea and the yellow pear
On and on and on I swim
Splashing both my hands and limbs
Look I think I see a bend,
And I think this is the end.

Sam Taggart (9)
Lowerhouse Junior School

SEASONS

Spring
Baby lambs are born
Dancing and skipping around the daisies.

Summer
Children play, screaming, running,
In bathing suits around the garden.

Autumn
Leaves fall off trees like confetti
Settling on the dark ground.

Winter
Snow settles on the houses
Children throw snowballs.

Lauren Watson-Walsh (10)
Lowerhouse Junior School

THE STARS

Up above the world so high
There is a sky,
That has stars
Right next to Mars,
Who ever is by my side
Those stars will be our guide.

Thomas Mawson
Lowerhouse Junior School

MY CAT

I have a pet cat,
That chases a rat,
When he sees a hole,
He goes to a fancy dress ball.

When he sees the mall,
He runs into the wall,
And when he sees a man,
He burns himself on a pan.

If you see my cat,
Please give it a pat,
Even though it is very fat,
Do you like my furry cat?

Hannah Camps (10)
Lowerhouse Junior School

SICK

'Mum, I don't want to go to school today
I feel sick and I think I should be away.
Mum, my head is hurting now
How can I stop it? How?
Mum, my legs are feeling very weak
I think I should stay off for a week.
Mum, my mind's all mixed up
Help Mum I'm puking up
Mum, please phone up school today'.
'But Sarah, it's Saturday!'

Wade Bond (9)
Lowerhouse Junior School

OH LITTLE SNAKEY

Once there was a big green snake,
Who slithered all the way down to the lake,
Looking for a juicy white egg.
Oh, what a silly mistake he has just made
For now the little snakey is dead.

Jade Barker (10)
Lowerhouse Junior School

SPRING

In spring beautiful white birds come and sing.
In spring I can see kites flying in the clear sky.
In spring people are excited.
In spring lambs jump and play.
In spring farmers grow food.
In spring people have picnics.
In spring I like to have fun.

Mudassar Mahmood (8)
Lomeshaye Junior School

SPRING

Spring is when multicoloured birds sing.
Spring is when birds say ting ting.
Spring is when beautiful flowers grow.
Spring is when we roar.
Spring is the best in the west.
Spring is when people spin in the sun.

Zairne Aslam (7)
Lomeshaye Junior School

SPRING

In spring I see beautiful birds singing in the trees.
In spring I see squirrels in the tree playing with their friends.
In spring I see fluffy, baby lambs.
In spring we play in the park and have a picnic too.
In spring there are blossoms on the trees.
In spring there are new green leaves on the trees.

Khafia Tufaul (7)
Lomeshaye Junior School

SPRING

In spring I see colourful birds singing.
In spring I see farmers getting food for the harvest.
In spring I see squirrels sitting.
In spring I see people in the park wearing shorts.
In spring I eat ice lollies.
In spring I go to the park with my uncle.

Humza Nawaz (7)
Lomeshaye Junior School

SPRING

In spring I can see people.
In spring I can see people flying kites.
In spring I can see nice flowers on the grass.
In spring I can see birds singing.
In spring I can see pretty leaves on the trees.
In spring I can see people eating ice cream.

Raheela Ahmed (7)
Lomeshaye Junior School

SPRING

Spring is when spotty birds come out
Spring is when the trees go green.
Spring is when farmers are harvesting.
Spring is when brown squirrels come out.
Spring is when birds sing.
Spring is when children play in the park.
Spring is when children have so much fun.

Sanam Ashraf
Lomeshaye Junior School

SPRING

In spring I can see a colourful butterfly.
In spring I can see a little bird singing in the tree so high.
In spring I can see a lovely clear blue sky.
In spring I can see lots of people flying kites.
In spring I can see lots of beautiful sights.

Sehrish Ismail
Lomeshaye Junior School

MY FUTURE

When I am older will there be a job left for me?
Will there be any food and drink left?
Will there be people left?
Will there be houses left for me?
What am I to do if everything is destroyed?

Maryam Jameela (9)
Lomeshaye Junior School

MY FRIENDS

Friends are kind,
Kind as ever.
Friends are playful,
Playful as ever.
Friends sing,
Friends dance,
Friends swim,
Friends are mad,
Friends go to school together,
Friends learn,
Friends are good,
Friends are forever.

Sahira Khurshid (8)
Lomeshaye Junior School

SPRING

High up in the sky colourful birds fly,
There are beautiful blossoms on trees,
Birds sit on branches and sing,
Little lambs jump in the field,
Hibernating animals come out to play,
Red and brown squirrels jump in the trees,
The sky is pale blue,
The clouds are smooth and fluffy,
Ducks swim in the pond calmly,
Farmers harvest and we eat lots of fruit,
I like spring.

Anam Elahi (7)
Lomeshaye Junior School

TREES

Trees are lovely and green
Especially when they're dry.

Trees are nice when they're different colours.

Trees are lovely in spring,
Autumn and summer.

Jackie Gregson (8)
Lomeshaye Junior School

STAR OF WONDER, STAR OF LIGHT

Star of wonder, star of light
I have a wish, a wish tonight
My wish will be a wish to the moon
And hope to see it soon.
When I see the moon shine bright
I see the world in black and white
Star of wonder, star of light
I have a wish, a wish tonight.

The next day
I was on the moon
It was really loud
Boom, boom, boom.
Then I saw a rocket
Flying past my head
Maybe I could like it on the moon
But I hope I'll be back home soon.

Louise Hocking (9)
Newchurch CE Primary School

MY FISH FRED

My fish called Fred
He's always in bed.

It looks like he's dead
He's got a little ted.

He looks like a duck
And his tank's full of muck.

He's chubby and stubby,
And like a Teletubbie.

Benjamin Bricknell (10)
Newchurch CE Primary School

PENCILS

Pencils in the sea, pencils on the ground,
When you scrape them on the table they make some sound.
Pencils on the floor, pencils through the door,
Pencils in the place where you lie some more.
Pencils in your room, pencils in the gloom,
Pencils in the place where you keep your broom.
Pencils in the bin, pencils in the tin,
Pencils in the place where you watch Tin Tin.
Pencils on the paper, pencils are good scrapers,
Pencils in the place where they labour people.

Lewis Fox (10)
Newchurch CE Primary School

DOGS

C ross-breeds are cute
O n the walk they pull you about
L ots of dogs are vicious
L ots of dogs are not
I myself think all dogs are cute
E nd of the day comes and they are all asleep.

B ulldogs are cute
U gly dogs are the ones I don't like
L ovely dogs are small
L ots of them like to play
D eadly dogs are scary
O ften they are playful
G ood dogs do not bite.

Chloe Nugent (9)
Newchurch CE Primary School

UNDER THE SEA

Under the sea where it's aqua blue
I saw a dolphin and a starfish too
Out came an octopus with its eight long legs
But then I saw a mother fish with her six little eggs.
I swam over the coral rock and my body spun around
And then I heard a killer whale's crying and moaning sound
But that was under the sea where it's aqua blue.

Ashlea Withey (10)
Newchurch CE Primary School

MY DOG SPOT

My dog Spot
He's full of snot
He chews on a pot
And he can tie a knot.

My dog Spot
He can fly
And one time
He nearly died.

My dog Spot
He's as daft as a dot
When he ate my hamster
I called him a disaster.

My dog Spot
He sleeps in a cot
Sometimes he has a piddle
So we call him Diddle.

Jordan Cattle (9)
Newchurch CE Primary School

THE TIDE

The tide is like a big water day
Roaring in and out
And when he's hungry he creates a tidal wave
So when he's vicious he sucks people down
Using a whirlpool to get its tea
You know he has a see-through body
Because you can see all the fish he has eaten.

Zak Sullivan (9)
Newchurch CE Primary School

ON MY WAY TO WORK

One early cold morning in London,
In 1924,
The mill owner comes out of the darkness,
To open the cotton mill door.

As I walk along the dim lit streets,
To my destination
There are lots of people waiting,
At the railway station.

I walk across the tower bridge,
The clock has just struck five
I don't want to go to work today
Cos gaffer will eat me alive.

I'll have to go to work today,
To get my weekly wages,
We won't be able to pay back our children's clothes
So they'll be in the naughty pages.

I run along the icy wet cobbles,
Turning a corner now and then;
Running on my way to work,
As I pass the farmer's chicken pen.

I can't believe I'm late for work today,
I never normally are;
Always hated work since I was small,
Rather hit myself with a bar.

My work is just around the corner,
Gaffer will be waiting there;
Oh I forgot work is closed for today,
Cos he's gone on holiday somewhere.

Calum Barrow (9)
Newchurch CE Primary School

IN MY BOX

In my box I would put . . .
The sound of brown leaves snapping off the tree.
The feel of grass blowing in the wind.
The sight of the shining sunshine.

The sound of waves crashing on the sand.
The feel of the sand running in my hands.
The sight of the clear blue sky.

Jake Nuttall (8)
St Anne's CE School, Rossendale

IN MY BOX

In my box I would put . . .
My shiny trophy that my brother gave me.
The sound of crashing wrestling to remind me what I'm going to be.
The sight of a heart to remind me that I've got a life.
The smell of deodorant to remind me of my house.
The taste of jelly to remind me of birthdays.
The sound of rappers singing and dancing.

Jordan Noon (8)
St Anne's CE School, Rossendale

IN MY BOX

In my box I would put . . .
The sound of the wind rushing on the hills.
The feel of soft grass with my fingertips.
The sight of the shiny sun setting.

In my box I would put . . .
The sound of the sand on the beach.
The feel of the sea coming on the sand.
The sight of the sun in the air.

Luke Evans (7)
St Anne's CE School, Rossendale

IN MY BOX

In my box I would put . . .
The sound of the wind blowing on my window.
The sight of the leaves falling off the trees.
The feel of the wind rushing through my hair.

The sound of the rain splashing in the puddles.
The sight of the raindrops hitting my car.
The freezing cold feeling of being soaking wet.

Craig Westerman (8)
St Anne's CE School, Rossendale

IN MY BOX

In my box I would put . . .
The sound of my family that I haven't seen since Christmas.
The touch of soft, velvety materials to think about my teddy.
The sight of the sea crashing against the sand.
The touch of my mum's skin, when I'm alone.
The sound of the wind rustling against the leaves.
The sight of the seagulls eating salmon.

Robyn Horrocks (9)
St Anne's CE School, Rossendale

IN MY BOX

In my box I would put . . .
The sound of owls hooting away at nightfall.
The sight of trees, swaying in the wind.
The feel of a soft furry rug lying near the fire.

In my box I would put . . .
The sound of laughter from my parents having fun.
The sight of my friends enjoying a party.
The feel of my lovely, cosy, comfy, squashy bed at night.

In my box I would put . . .
The sound of the pages of a book turning over and over.
The sight of people climbing up Seat Naze.
The feel of warm skin on my cold bare hands.

In my box I would put . . .
The sound of birds whistling in the sunshine.
The sight of ice glistening like diamonds.
The feel of silk like my pyjamas.

Tiffany Holt (9)
St Anne's CE School, Rossendale

IN MY BOX

In my box I would put . . .
The sound of the gentle wind blowing the flowers.
The feel of a silky shell on my feet.
The sight of a beautiful dolphin leaping up and down.

The sound of the waves crashing on the beach.
The feel of the sand trickling through my fingers.
The sight of a beautiful picture of my mummy and daddy.

Fern Toman (8)
St Anne's CE School, Rossendale

IN MY BOX

In my box I would put . . .
The sound of the wind whistling on windy days.
The feel of a teddy that's furry and soft.
The sight of the sunset that's pink and orange.

The sound of racing cars going really fast.
The feel of feathers soft and smooth.
The sight of ducks floating along.

The sound of birds tweeting.
The feel of cotton wool on my fingertips.
The sight of a sunny beach.

Kane Irving (7)
St Anne's CE School, Rossendale

THE WATERFALL

The waterfall is sparkling
It sparkles with glee
It is beautiful,
Looks fantastic,
It's brilliant.
You look around
There are little fish
That are in the bottom
That looks like a dish
The fish are golden orange.

Rachel Holland (9)
St James' CE Primary School, Clitheroe

THE WATERFALL

Flowing fall,
Shining blue.
Please shine,
Please shine,
Please flow
For me,
Do not stop now,
Please flow on and on forever.

Deborah O'Reilly (8)
St James' CE Primary School, Clitheroe

A RIDDLE

I am white and cold and round
But I am not a clock
So what am I?

I am not a snowball
You might see me at night.

Answer - the moon.

Amber Bateman (8)
St James' CE Primary School, Clitheroe

GOODNIGHT POEM

Goodnight, goodnight,
Switch off the light,
You might have a nightmare,
But you will have a fright!

Nikkita Everett (8)
St James' CE Primary School, Clitheroe

DINNER RIDDLE

You use me at dinner time
Before you go to bed
And you use us to pick up from mouth to head.
One of me is long and sharp and the other is like four darts
We're like a type of equipment, like a type of force
And there's two of us of course!
And there's one more thing before you go
That I am sure all of you will want to know
I am a knife and fork!

Samuel Ismail (8)
St James' CE Primary School, Clitheroe

RIDDLE

I'm big and beautiful,
I'm a predator,
I fly all day,
Can you guess who I am?

Answer - eagle.

Joe Swierczynski (8)
St James' CE Primary School, Clitheroe

THE SNOWMAN

The snowman has a hat on,
He always plays the games,
You play every day he's there
He's always a happy snowman
Until the day he melts.

Mollie Webber (8)
St James' CE Primary School, Clitheroe

MY ACROSTIC POEM

S nowflakes
N ever settle
O n
W et boots
F rost is freezing
L ake is frosty
A nd people fly
K ites over it
E nd!

Rachel Stevens (8)
St James' CE Primary School, Clitheroe

DO YOU WANT TO GO UP THERE?

Do you want to go up there?
Go and float in the air,
Go and float like a bird,
Do you want to go up there?
Do you?
I do.

Francesca Green (8)
St James' CE Primary School, Clitheroe

THE SPIDER WEB

The spider climbs the web
The spider is creepy and black
He's creepy in your house.

Sophie Cox (8)
St James' CE Primary School, Clitheroe

RIDDLE

I am round,
I am hard,
I am something that you kick around.

Every week I get kicked,
Five or ten times,
When it rains I shout 'Yippee!'

Answer - football.

Conor Banki-Williamson (7)
St James' CE Primary School, Clitheroe

RIDDLE

I might be brown or grey
I like to live in your house
I may like cheese
But I'm not a mouse
Who am I?

Answer - rat.

Ryan Hargreaves (9)
St James' CE Primary School, Clitheroe

VIKINGS

Vikings are very brave
They surf up and down all day
They settle wherever they can find
Trying to get more energy
And back they go!

Charlie Kane (7)
St Joseph's RC Primary School, Todmorden

WHAT A LOVELY DAY

What a lovely day
The dry sand is as rough
As sandpaper tickling my feet.

What a lovely day
The wet sand is as silky
As hamsters fur.

What a lovely day
The rocks are as hot
As fire burning my feet when I stand on them.

What a lovely day
The seaweed is as slimy
As a dog's nose.

What a lovely day
The sea is as blue
As the sky drifting over me.

Jordan Goldie (10)
St Joseph's RC Primary School, Todmorden

THE BUG PARADE

One night a year the bugs come down
From the hills and to the ground
They sing and dance in the moonlit sky
I'm telling the truth it's not a lie.

Now it's time for the bug parade
They're wearing costumes they have made
From soft cloth to a dirty old jacket
They don't care just make a racket.

It's getting late, house lights go out
Now's not the time to sing and shout
Now's the time to go to sleep
But lots of memories they will keep.

Christina Roche (10)
St Joseph's RC Primary School, Todmorden

THE FLYING DUTCHMAN

I was sailing across the ocean
But with no commotion
I was sailing on and on
With my ship The Son
Then it was foggy
And I saw my doggy
Then I saw a wrecked ship
Which gave me a shiver in my hip
The ship was floating on the ocean
With a rocking motion
I climbed aboard the haunted ship
It was so big I felt like a pip
Then I heard a voice saying 'Get lost'
Then I felt something as cold as frost
I saw a headless ghost
Tied against a post
I was running for my life
The ghost threw a knife
The knife missed me
And fell into the sea
I climbed back into The Son
And sailed on and on
I saw the ship go back to the seabed
The ship said The Flying Dutchman.

Paul Williams (11)
St Joseph's RC Primary School, Todmorden

SEASIDE

The sea crashes onto the land
As smooth as walking on the sand
The sea is as blue as the sky
And then you can see the birds fly
The sea is as beautiful as a picture on a wall
And as beautiful as a carpet on the floor
The sea is gorgeous it smells ravishing
And looks dazzling.

Thomas Wadsworth (11)
St Joseph's RC Primary School, Todmorden

SANTA

S   anta goes around at night
A   nd it's only once a year
N   othing can stop him now
T   ill day dawns
A   fter that he goes to bed until next year.

Callum Hall (7)
St Joseph's RC Primary School, Todmorden

SANTA

S   anta goes around at night
A   nd nothing can stop him
N   ight must be dark but he takes a torch
T   aking his pets for a ride
A   man taking presents to people.

Jim Frain (8)
St Joseph's RC Primary School, Todmorden

I Wish I Could Swim With Dolphins

The dolphins leap up and down through the crystal clear sea
They talk and leap and swim
They swim with fishes.

Oh I wish I could swim with dolphins!

They talk and swim,
They dive and swoop,
The sun glistens on their slippy backs like crystals,
They're playful,
They're kind,
They're lovely,
They love humans
And they're cheerful.

Oh I wish I could swim with dolphins!

Jodie-Louise Kane (10)
St Joseph's RC Primary School, Todmorden

Angel

Wings as gold and sparkly as the sun
Crown as jewelled as the stars at night
Cloak as long as a human's life
Dress as bright as Heaven
Lips as red as a drop of blood
Skin as smooth and warm hearted as God's heart
Eyes as blue as the sea
Hair as smooth and rich as the sand
Wings made from silk
Delicately made from spider's webs.

Lilian McGroarty (10)
St Joseph's RC Primary School, Todmorden

WHY?

Why does the rain always drop on me?
Why does the wind blow my hat off?
Why does the wind blow my kite?
Why does the snow come?
Why do people make snowmen?
Why do people throw snowballs at me?
Do you know it Mum?

Matthew Crowley (8)
St Joseph's RC Primary School, Todmorden

ROCKETS

R   ockets can fly high, high, high
O   ver the stars, over the moon
C   alling 'Hello, hello' to
K   ate, calling 'Hello, hello' back
E   nemy aliens always come
T   rying to go from star to star.

Joshua Dolan (8)
St Joseph's RC Primary School, Todmorden

STAR

Star, star is so bright
It gets bigger every night
It might be there tonight
The star you see every night
Has been placed there for our delight!

Jenny Bentley (7)
St Joseph's RC Primary School, Todmorden

FOOTBALL

F   ootball is the best
O   n the ball all the time
O   n the ball for a shot
T   ill the goalkeeper takes the ball off you
B   ecause he can't let you score
A   nd you are a striker you shoot the ball and score
L   ight is your second name
L   ight is on your T-shirt,
            Then the referee blows the whistle for full-time
            'We win' you shout.

Conor Armstrong (9)
St Joseph's RC Primary School, Todmorden

SNAKES SLIDE

They slide around in the polar pound
When the snakes hiss
The bears might give them a kiss.

Kurt Thorne (8)
St Joseph's RC Primary School, Todmorden

MY AUNTY JANE

My Aunty Jane came on a train
She hit me with a cane, then it started to rain
She called me a big pain.

William Lord (8)
St Joseph's RC Primary School, Todmorden

THE BEST SPACE

The best place
Is in space
In a rocket
Quick lock it
Put it in a pocket
Plug it in the socket
Going out
Flowing out
Blowing out
Seeing Mars
Looking at stars
Got to stop
Get the mop
Plop killed
Let's grill it
Put it in the till
Have a birthday in space
It's the best place for you!

Hannah Quigley (9)
St Joseph's RC Primary School, Todmorden

MY GUINEA PIG

My guinea pig's cuddly
My guinea pig's sweet.
Sometimes she jumps over my feet.

I play with her every day and feed her twice too
Sometimes she stares at me or at you.

When she smells hay she goes crazy
When we bath her she jumps on me and I get soaked.

Helena Landau (8)
St Joseph's RC Primary School, Todmorden

CHRISTMAS

C   hristmas is great
H   appy Christmas
R   eindeers come
I   n the night
S   leep tight
T   hen they come
M   ight come
A   nd bring me presents
S   leep tight in the night.

Siobhan Ingham (8)
St Joseph's RC Primary School, Todmorden

BOOMERANG

Boomerang
Backwards
And forwards
This way and that
Look out!
The boomerang's about.

Ruth Wadsworth (8)
St Joseph's RC Primary School, Todmorden

PLANETS

Planets, planets in space
You might see Planet Shoelace.
Planets, planets in the air
Be excited, we're nearly there.

Nathan Ashman
St Joseph's RC Primary School, Todmorden

BEACH

'I want to go to the beach today, so I can play
I need to go to the beach today, so I can lay on the beach.
I'll walk to the beach today, so I can collect my cockle shells.
I'll run to the beach today, I have to do my way today.
Please can I go to the beach today, please, please'.

'No way!'

Laura Sharrock (10)
St Joseph's RC Primary School, Todmorden

THE HAUNTED HOUSE

The curtains are like old rags blowing in the gentle breeze.
The floorboards creak like mice crying for help.
The door slams, it is like getting slapped by your mum.
The ghosts scare you like your friends do
                                when they sneak up behind you.

Charlotte Agley (10)
St Joseph's RC Primary School, Todmorden

LIQUORICE

My little cat is black and fat
And never comes out and plays
He sleeps all day and is out all night
And eats his favourite dish
That's fish.

Sam Tonkinson (9)
St Joseph's RC Primary School, Todmorden

GRANDAD

Based on a real grandad.

I love my grandad very much,
I miss your loving caring touch,
I miss your kind and gentle face,
But now you're in a better place.

I love my grandad very much,
I miss your cuddles oh so much,
Now that you have passed away,
Your heart is here to stay.

You come down from Heaven above,
And also send your caring love,
You never had a dream come true,
That's why this poem is meant for you.

Shavon Pointon (10)
St Joseph's RC Primary School, Todmorden

FOOTY MAD

Come on you reds
The people shout, the babies scream
Robbie Fowler fouls other people
Shearer scores far through the air
Trying to catch its power
Mud flying through the air
Goal! Goal! Goal!
The crowd shouts
Goal is all they say for now!

James Baker (9)
St Joseph's RC Primary School, Todmorden

FATHER CHRISTMAS

F   ather Christmas gives us presents
A   nd lots and lots of sweets and treats
T   he reindeers lead the way
H   e is very jolly
E   very day
R   udolf is always glad to play.

C   hristmas tree is up already
H   igh up in the sky they fly
R   ing, ring the Christmas bells
I   n and out the towns they go
S   o it snows every year
T   oday is full of fun and cheer
'M erry Christmas' he says
A   nd I love Christmas dinner
S   o do I love all my presents.

Amy Rez (8)
St Joseph's RC Primary School, Todmorden

IN THE CLASS AND AT HOME

Sir said 'Sit down!'
'Children don't give me a frown!'
He says he is mad!
Oh he is really sad!
Oh my sister is really cute!
My big sister plays the flute!
My dad's car horn goes Toot! Toot! Toot!
We have a cat called Fluff.
My little sister's train goes puff.

Lauren Gelling (9)
St Joseph's RC Primary School, Todmorden

SCUBA-DIVING

S un is shining and I go down to the aqua pool
C ar is lovely and big for my equipment
U ran is my scuba-diving instructor
B ob the demonstrator shows me what to do
A quick change out of clothes on goes my scuba stuff.

D iving is cool and brill the air tank weighs a ton
I dive into the pool with a splash
V inny my mate came down to the bottom after me
I paddle like mad up and down the pool like a shark
N ine metres down in the pool
G ena's generator starts in the pool.

Daniel Lively (9)
St Joseph's RC Primary School, Todmorden

MEET THE FAMILY

We're green, we're mean, we're from out of space
This is Mum, she's really fun and brill at making tea.
This is Dad, he's very bad and he loves to make a mess
He's a pain in the bum but he still loves Mum for some reason
                                        out of this world.
This is Milly she's really silly
She prances about all day
She bugs me for fun and lies to our mum and always gets her own way.
They're all OK but at the end of the day
I like myself the best.

Lauren Griffiths (10)
St Joseph's RC Primary School, Todmorden

OLD ABANDONED PARK

In the old abandoned park where squirrels hide their nuts in grass
It's a mystery why they run and hide
When leaves go rustling by
But when the heat dies and night falls
The animals flee
They all know they have got company
At midnight bright lights flash
A billion shadows should be seen by crescent moon
But no one comes across the abandoned park
What comes across the abandoned park?

No one knows!

Tim Waite (10)
St Joseph's RC Primary School, Todmorden

FLYING ALL OVER THE WORLD

Flying, flying
Through space
Zooming! Zooming!
All over the place
Looking at Mars and stars,
Space jets going,
Going, never going to stop.
Oooh! I hope we stop some time
Crash! Bang! Wallop!
Oh no! We're on Mars!
Ahhhh!

Katie Suthers (8)
St Joseph's RC Primary School, Todmorden

MY FAMILY TREE

My family tree is the best
My family tree is the greatest
My family tree is better than your family tree
My family has . . .

Grandma and Grandad
Mum and Dad
Tony, me and Natasha,
Auntie Leah and Aiden
Auntie Dawn, Guy,
Samantha and Anthony.

Tammy Ross (8)
St Joseph's RC Primary School, Todmorden

THE SEASIDE

I love going to the seaside
The sea is nice and wide
The sand is as brown as chocolate ice cream
And the sea is as if it will make you scream
My friends say that if I cry
The sea will quickly pass by
My feet might sink in the sand
And so will my rubber hair band
I'd jump in the sea
But I have to go for my tea!

Jessica Gill (10)
St Joseph's RC Primary School, Todmorden

WHAT AM I?

I go for walks and I always play
I wag my tail and grab the mail
I am always sleepy when I come back from my walks
I am always weepy when I've been playing
Then I'm always saying to myself
To go and dig a bone
But it's not fair I'm all alone
I chase cats and sit on my mats
And go to sleep all night.

Vicky Markiewicz (10)
St Joseph's RC Primary School, Todmorden

PET POLITICS

The magistrate's a hamster!
The judge is a dog!
The jury are all cats!
My lawyer is a hog!
The defendant is a snake!
The crowd are all mongoose!
The guard is a worm!
The picture makes us squirm!
The termites give us bites!
The judge loves mice!
The cats hate head lice!
The monkeys are precise!
The cows eat lice!

Michael Hardman (9)
St Mary's RC Primary School, Rossendale

THE RUNAWAY DOG

There was a dog called Patch,
Who always tried to open his hatch
He had an owner who was very small
She always took him to Townley Hall
She fed him peanut butter and jam
But Patch didn't eat this, he only ate ham.

Sadly Patch had to go to the vets
But he was very happy because he met some other pets.

When it was his turn to go in
The vet said Patch looked very thin
He looked Patch's case up in his book
'You've got a case of the wild berry jam hook'
His owner asked the vet 'Is he allergic to lamb?'
'No' laughed the vet 'I'm afraid it's the ham.'
Patch squealed, barked and cried
His owner only looked at Patch and sighed.

On the way home Patch ran away
For he couldn't stay another day
He lived on wild berries, grass and trees
Eventually he ran home because of the bees
Because he'd got used to wild berries, grass and trees,
His owner understood Patch's needs.

Every day after that
Patch's owner would give him a pat
She'd whip up some berries and grass
And she would take him to midnight mass
After that Patch didn't open his hatch
He'd stay inside and play some catch.

Francesca Lovell (9)
St Mary's RC Primary School, Rossendale

ANIMALS

Animals and their habitats,
Monstrous wolves to big cats,
Enormous hogs,
And cute little dogs.
Some live in a house,
With a little mouse,
They have lots of toys,
And like to play with boys.

They love to eat,
When their food tastes sweet,
Some live in trees,
And rustle in leaves.
Birds like to sing,
While the lion prowls and says he's king,
Hamsters, gerbils, everything
And ducks with wings.

They squawk and squeak
And like to speak
But even if some are pests
Animals will always be the best.

Laura Holden (9)
St Mary's RC Primary School, Rossendale

ANIMALS IN THE ZOO

Tigers are ferocious, bears are much the same!
I can't say much for leopards because they have no fame!
But many, many animals are very, very lame!
Most sloths are very tame!

Niall Misell (9)
St Mary's RC Primary School, Rossendale

A FRIEND OF A FRIEND

Freddy the frog
Lived on a log
He had many friends
Like Danny the dog.

Danny the dog
Loved to live in a house,
Had many friends
Like Minnie the mouse.

Minnie the mouse
Lived in a box,
She had many friends
Like Frankie the fox.

Frankie the fox
Lived in a bush
He had many friends
Like Thrilly the thrush.

Thrilly the thrush
Lived in a nest,
She had a friend
Like the rest.

I just say this friend,
Is one of the best
Her friend is Jesus
Did you guess?

Celia O'Keefe (10)
St Mary's RC Primary School, Rossendale

MY CAT

She is called Sox,
She plays in a box.
With her face which is white,
She looks a cute little mite.
When it is sunny,
She is so playful and funny.
She's got four sweet little paws,
And when she gets teased she shows her claws.
She likes scratching the mat,
That's my cat!

Ashden Higgins (8)
St Mary's RC Primary School, Rossendale

MY TEACHER

My teacher, she's the worst
Especially when she keeps us under that awful curse
When that ruler hits the desk
Crash!
As dead as a doorbell.

My teacher, she's the worst
Especially when she gets hold of my purse
Gone
All my savings gone.

My teacher, she's the best
Now she wears that old string vest
That smells of rotten bread and has huge holes in
But still she's the best.

Fiona Tormey (10)
St Mary's RC Primary School, Sabden

DIAMOND ISLAND

Bang! The saucy ship had docked on an island
Known as the Diamond Island,
The crew saw blazing sun for the first time in days
But there was something strange,
Now they would call the place
Cartoon Island.
The ship was big, the island was small,
The sailors thought the rocks were tall.
The strong sailors
Were scared
A giant rubber was rubbing everything out
The rubber was rubbing,
The men were running.
The captain said 'Hurry up!'
The men where just in time,
But one little boy he was all rubbed out,
And now named Mr Nobody
The ship was big, the island was small,
The sailors thought the rocks were tall.

Joseph Keane (9)
St Mary's RC Primary School, Sabden

MISS TAYLOR

Miss Taylor, Miss Taylor
She dresses like a queen
And she never, never, ever
Shouts at me and she giggles with glee.

She dresses like a queen
Every day of the queen week.

Melanie Hamer (9)
St Mary's RC Primary School, Sabden

CUSTARD MOUNTAIN

Custard Mountain's hard to find,
But if you do it's worth it,
It's full of custard, it's very strange,
It's sticky and hot with sherbet!

Custard Mountain, Custard Mountain
I love you so much!

In other words, it's Heaven!
For children of our age,
The sticky golden syrup,
Oozes out at full rage.

Custard Mountain, Custard Mountain
I love you so much!

It's totally sweet,
And I've been there once before,
I had to come back though,
Even now, I still want some more!

Custard Mountain, Custard Mountain
I love you so much!

Maria Keane (11)
St Mary's RC Primary School, Sabden

CATS

There was a cat, it had a purple hat
And it was very fat.
The cat was very fat because it sits on the mat
The cat was very mad and very sad
And the cat was too fat.

Liam Smith (9)
St Mary's RC Primary School, Sabden

THE FIREWORK

I am a firework
Ready to go,
Strike a match,
Light a fuse
And I go boom in the sky.

Bang! Bang!
Colours of the rainbow,
Purple, green and yellow.

I am a firework
Stuck in the ground,
They light a fuse,
And I go whee like a rocket.

I go boom! The colours explode everywhere,
I am below the sparkling stars,
I am below the shining moon
And the midnight sky.

Joseph Wilkins (10)
St Mary's RC Primary School, Sabden

FOOD

I love food, I love pasta,
I love chocolate, I love apples,
I love sweets, I love food!

I hate beans, I hate mashed potatoes,
I hate pizza, I hate peas,
I hate oranges,
But I love everything else.

Luke Pissochet (8)
St Mary's RC Primary School, Sabden

THE JELLY MAN

I went to the desert in Egypt city
Had no water, oh what a pity
I met a fat man he was very smelly
He said 'What are you looking at, my yummy jelly?'
He grabbed me by my neck and said,
'You can't have it, it's too smelly!
I'm gonna squash your little belly,'
I said 'No sir don't squash me
I'm too young to die you see.'
'All right lad you're a cool guy,
Walk right home.' Oh I hate goodbyes.

Thomas Fitzpatrick (10)
St Mary's RC Primary School, Sabden

IN SPACE

In space the moon sparkles
Like a shining diamond
The sun is like a thousand comets
Pluto is like a million fridge freezers
Freezing everything on it
Mercury is like huge furnace sizzling in the solar system
Comets are like huge fireballs
Whizzing past all the planets
Earth is the planet of the human race
Orbiting the sun night and day
Stars sit proudly near the planets gleaming in the darkness.

Adam Bradley (10)
St Mary's RC Primary School, Sabden

CATS

Open the door and what do you see?
I see a cat in a hat
That's what I see.

Open the door and what do you see?
I see a fat rat
That's what I see.

Open the door and what do you see?
I see a cat in a hat and a fat rat
That's what I see.

Open the door and what do you see?
I see a grinning Cheshire cat smiling at me
That's what I see.

Open the door and what do you see?
Nothing but me.

Emma Bromley (8)
St Mary's RC Primary School, Sabden

A SHIP AT SEA

Marvellous pink, smelling absolutely divine corridors
Like a sparkly massive huge wave heading towards the shore
Like a dog with a horrendous bone,
That sparkles in the sunlight.
Like a sunset in the wind
The crinkles of the beautiful sea
Is the wooden planks of wood,
A shine of the finest diamonds
A twinkle in the sky
As quiet as a cemetery.

Rosie Wain (8)
St Mary's RC Primary School, Sabden

I THOUGHT I SAW . . .

I thought I saw . . .
I thought I saw . . .
An adventurous place beyond the world,
Filled with colours and delight.
What a beautiful sight.

I looked in my pond
And I thought I saw . . .
A beautiful sea world
Then I saw an eel all round and curled
It looked like a kite.
What a beautiful sight.

I looked in my garden
And I thought I saw . . .
A huge jungle with trees and leaves,
With tigers and lions and monkeys and leopards.
What a beautiful sight.

When I looked in the bush
I thought I saw . . .
Wait it's going all blurry
It was all just a dream,
Oh well at least I can dream.
What a beautiful dream.

Stephanie Edwards (9)
St Mary's RC Primary School, Sabden

CRAZY LITTLE DOG

There was a dog, a crazy little dog,
He ate our house,
He ate a train,
He's a real pain.
He ate a school,
Oh what a fool, that crazy little dog.

My mum couldn't put up with it
She threw him in the bin
I miss that crazy little dog
Although he ate a train and is a pain
Oh what a fool, that crazy little dog.

Geraldine McKavanagh (8)
St Mary's RC Primary School, Sabden

MY TEACHER

My teacher is kind,
My teacher is nice,
My teacher sometimes smells of spice.

My teacher is happy,
My teacher is sweet,
My teacher likes us to do our work neat.

My teacher is clever,
My teacher is smart,
My teacher is very good at art.

My teacher is loud,
My teacher is out,
My teacher can hear us, eek can she shout!

Kim Fish (9)
St Michael & All Angels CE Primary School, Colne

THE DAY I GOT MY CAT

The day I went to the pet shop,
I went looking for a cat.
My mum said 'We should rescue one,'
I didn't argue with that.

So when I went inside,
I found the one for me,
We took her home in the car,
Sitting on my knee.

Bethany Dyson (9)
St Michael & All Angels CE Primary School, Colne

SPACE

A planet is like a face
But in space.
An astronaut on the moon,
Looks like a cartoon.
On Earth you can see stars,
You can see even more on Mars.
The Earth is blue and green,
Jupiter's giant red spot is like a bean.

Josh Titley (9)
St Michael & All Angels CE Primary School, Colne

MY MUM IS MAD ABOUT MARSHMALLOWS

My mum is mad about marshmallows,
She eats them day and night,
I just can't believe that she can stand the lot,
Oh I give up if she takes another bite.

Chelsea Singleton (8)
St Michael & All Angels CE Primary School, Colne

THE VOLCANO

I am a big volcano
Who has been asleep for a while
But I can feel a rumbling
Deep down below.

The people who live near me
Are starting to gather their things
They can feel a rumbling
And hear strange things.

I wouldn't mean to hurt them
When I spit my lava out
It's like I feel unwell
And better when it's out.

I can feel it bubbling
It's getting hotter and hotter
The grumbling inside me is getting louder
There is steam coming out of my top.

At last I am ready
The lava is flowing out
I feel so much better
Now all the sizzling lava is thrown out.

Now it is all over
The people are coming back
I feel so much better, very tired too
Now I can go back to sleep for another year or two.

Laura Widdup (8)
St Michael & All Angels CE Primary School, Colne

WHEN I FIRST MADE FRIENDS

When I first made friends,
These friends were really nice.
When I first made friends,
These friends smelt of sugar spice.

My first friend was Charlotte,
My second friend was Emily.
I don't know why I chose Emily,
Because it was really Bethany.

We all played outside together,
Because it was playtime.

Elizabeth Cox (8)
St Michael & All Angels CE Primary School, Colne

ALL ABOUT ME

My name is Jak and I am a boy
I always play with my toy
I have a dad that is very kind
He lets my mum out and he doesn't mind
Mum is nice
Because she let Craig round twice
My dad is cool
Because he works at a big boys' school
And that is me
Oops! I have to have my tea!

Jak Carradice (8)
St Michael & All Angels CE Primary School, Colne

GERBILS

G erbils scutter here and there,
E ating greedily without a care,
R ummaging in their food, they like it such a lot,
B urrowing in their bed to find their favourite spot,
I n and out of their cardboard tubes,
L eaping off their wooden cube,
S ometimes at night they make lots of noise!

Emily Jayne Lee (8)
St Michael & All Angels CE Primary School, Colne

WINTER

W ind is beating on my face,
I cicles hanging on my roof,
N ever being warm at all,
T rees that have no leaves,
E veryone having snowball fights in the snow,
R ecords playing Christmas carols.

Kyle Wimbles (8)
St Michael & All Angels CE Primary School, Colne

SPACE

S aturn is a planet with many rings
P luto feels so very cold
A liens are there or so we're told
C raters deep and maybe sea
E arth is home to you and me.

Charlotte Percival (9)
St Michael & All Angels CE Primary School, Colne

MY SISTER

My sister is so sweet
She likes to chew her feet
She never does what she is told
But she is six months old!

Her name is Alexia Grace
She's always dressed in lace
She is a lovely girl
And has one curl.

My sister likes to laugh
When she is in the bath
She likes to hold on tight
When you kiss her goodnight.

My sister is always happy
Unless you change her nappy
You never hear her cry
And likes to wave goodbye.

Cory Howarth
St Michael & All Angels CE Primary School, Colne

ALL ALONE

All alone I sit at night,
Watching all the stars shine bright.
Wishing and wishing all night through,
I hope my wishing will come true.

When I wake and see the light,
And the sunshine shining bright.
I know my wishing has come true,
When I see the sunshine shining through.

Layla Birtwistle (9)
St Michael & All Angels CE Primary School, Colne

WINTER

W hen it is snowing I always play out
I cicles hard and soft hang from roofs
N ow it is Christmas, Jesus' birth
T ender fingers of snow and icicles
E verywhere white all covered in snow
R obins hopping and jumping around.

Craig Wiseman (8)
St Michael & All Angels CE Primary School, Colne

WINTER

W inter means snow
I n my home I get ready
N ow outside snowball in my hand
T oo cold to play out anymore
E ating my hot tea
R eady for bed.

Luke Hardy (9)
St Michael & All Angels CE Primary School, Colne

SLOTHS

S loths going slow
L eaves rustling
O h so slowly, oh so slow
T rees trembling as they go
H ere come sloths.

Ruth French (8)
St Michael & All Angels CE Primary School, Colne

SNOW

Snow is bright,
Snow is white,
We all enjoy a snowball fight.

We'll build a snowman
And get cold toes,
We'll use coal for eyes,
And a carrot for the nose.

It's snowing,
Our fingers are glowing,
Inside we sit by the fire,
The flames getting higher.

The lake has frozen,
The children skate,
Get off the ice,
Before it's too late.

Alexander Shorrock (8)
St Michael & All Angels CE Primary School, Colne

MY MOUSE

I had a mouse
It lived in my doll's house
I tucked it up in my doll's bed
I gave it breakfast in bed.

I looked after him well
I gave him baths every day
His name is Mr Happy
And he's my favourite little mousey.

Emily Birtwell (9)
St Michael & All Angels CE Primary School, Colne

THE WALL WENT CRACK

Humpty Dumpty sat on the wall
Because he was so fat the wall went crack.
All the king's horses and all the king's men
Couldn't put the wall back up again.

Humpty Dumpty had a bad head
So he went home and got into bed.
While he was asleep snoozing away,
His headache cleared and he felt OK.

Amy Monaghan (9)
St Michael & All Angels CE Primary School, Colne

THE TIRED TEACHER

The tired teacher
Works all day
Marking our book in
An untidy way.

The tired teacher
Tries his best
Never has time to
Have a rest.

The tired teacher
Says 'Stop, stop, stop'
Shout out loud
'I'll blow my top'.

Dionne Ashworth Howorth (11)
St Peter's CE Primary School, Accrington

TIMOTHY

Timothy, Timothy
Yellow and red
Mum shouted
Get to bed.

Timothy, Timothy
Blue and green
You've never seen him
Be so mean.

Timothy, Timothy
Purple and blue
When you look at him
He will say I love you.

Timothy, Timothy
Couldn't tell time
Timothy, Timothy
He is mine.

Timothy, Timothy
Has just died
Timothy, Timothy
Everyone cried.

Timothy, Timothy
Is my friend,
Timothy, Timothy
This is the end.

Shaista Hussain (10)
St Peter's CE Primary School, Accrington

CHIMNEY SWEEP

Chimney sweep, chimney sweep has no fun
Chimney sweep, chimney sweep longs to see the sun.

Chimney sweep, chimney sweep has low pay
Chimney sweep, chimney sweep works hard all day.

Chimney sweep, chimney sweep no time to rest
Chimney sweep, chimney sweep no time to joke
No time to jest.

Chimney sweep, chimney sweep covered in soot
Chimney sweep, chimney sweep with bruises from head to foot.

Chimney sweep, chimney sweep what a horrible job.

Bronwyn Stirzaker (11)
St Peter's CE Primary School, Accrington

THE SUN

The sun is a yellow coiled snake squeezing its prey.
It's an orange ball floating in the sky.
A glowing shining soul drifting away.
It is a gold burning rock stranded in the sky.
It is a big bright flaming fire in the moonlit sky.
A reflecting light in the deep dark night.
A golden shining cup and saucer.
It is the middle of a flower swaying from side to side.
It is a tasty yellow gobstopper.
It is a big round magic mirror.
It is a gold Christmas bauble.

The sun.

Emma Archer (10)
St Peter's CE Primary School, Accrington

THE TIRED TEACHER

Tired teacher,
Tired teacher
We're wasting his time
But he's making us cry
Never time for break
He's always trying to make us work.

Tired teacher,
Tired teacher
Correcting our mistakes
Never time for break
He says like always
Now it's time to go home
Hooray!

He's got a banging headache,
His face is red,
His ears are steaming,
Boom!
That was his head
Is he dead?

Lauren Beaumont (10)
St Peter's CE Primary School, Accrington

BLUE

Blue is the colour of the bad card box
Blue is the colour of my green socks.

Blue is the colour of the calculator in school
Blue is the colour of the richest jewel.

Blue is the colour that everyone likes
Blue is the colour of my blue bike.

Blue is the colour of my inside-out coat
Blue is the colour of my blue boat.

Blue is the colour of my pencil case
Blue is the colour of my old lace.

Ricky Gudgeon (11)
St Peter's CE Primary School, Accrington

WINTER

Winter, winter you're my best friend
I wish you would never end.
Outside it is snowing
People are snowballing
Building snowmen in the thick snow
Makes our faces start to glow
'Come inside' my mother said
'Have some hot chocolate then go to bed'.

Soaib Khan (10)
St Peter's CE Primary School, Accrington

ME, MYSELF, I, MINE

Bright blue eyes,
Light brown hair,
Fashionable clothes I love to wear.
I like to travel,
I love to play,
I always like to get my own way.
This is me, this is I, this is myself
This is mine.

Laura Whittaker (10)
St Peter's CE Primary School, Accrington

THE TIRED TEACHER

The tired teacher sometimes shouts
I bet he feels like giving us a clout.

The tired teacher is so kind
I bet he has a real good mind.

We do the maths he does the marking
When he shouts it's like a dog barking.

He tried his best every single day
And really looks forward to his weekly pay.

Jacob Sledden (11)
St Peter's CE Primary School, Accrington

THE SUN

The sun is shining, blazing hot
Like a comfy baby's cot.

The sun is like a gold king's ring
Every time I play out it shines on my swing.

The sun is a yellow floating ball
It shines on people big and small.

The sun is round, round, round, round,
Honestly I don't know where it was found.

Saria Akhtar (11)
St Peter's CE Primary School, Accrington

GOLD

Gold is the colour
Of the money I save.
Gold is the treasure
In dark, dark cave.

Gold is the colour
Of my best pen.
Gold is the feet
And beak of a hen.

Gold is the colour
Of the eagle's eye.
Gold is the sun
In the deep blue sky.

Gold is the colour
Of shining money.
Gold is the colour
Of sweet, yellow honey.

Gold is the colour
Of a special ring.
Gold is the crown
Of a powerful king.

Gold is the colour
Of a delicious egg yolk.
Gold is the property
Of wealthy folk.

Gold is the colour
Of a princesses' ball.
Gold is the best colour
Of them all.

Lita Lord (10)
St Peter's CE Primary School, Accrington

JACK FROST IN THE DARK

Shhh! Shhh!
Jack Frost is around!
Creeping up the stairs
Crystals somewhere!
Hiding! Sneaking!
Hiding under there!

Beware! Beware!
Of Jack Frost!
Chasing him everywhere!
Round the bend!
Over my head!
He sped somewhere!

Over the bushes,
Over the grass,
Everything goes white
Stay away!
In the dark
Of the night!

Matthew Allen (9)
St Veronica's RC Primary School, Rossendale

RAINBOW

Red, orange, yellow and green
It's a special rainbow that I have seen
Blue, indigo and violet
In a rainbow there is no pilot
Although the rainbow is so beautiful
It soon fades away
And will come back another day.

Laura Starkie (8)
St Veronica's RC Primary School, Rossendale

SILVER FROST

Jack Frost! Jack Frost!
Like a snake.
Jack Frost! Jack Frost! Jack Frost!
Jack Frost! Jack Frost!
Sneaky, wicked,
He's got it in for you!

Jack Frost! Jack Frost!
He's here! He's there!
Jack Frost! Jack Frost! Jack Frost!
Jack Frost! Jack Frost!
Crafty, evil,
Hardening and whitening the grass.

Jack Frost! Jack Frost!
Creepy, haunting,
Jack Frost! Jack Frost! Jack Frost!
Jack Frost! Jack Frost!
Devious, mean,
Casting his spell through the world.

Daniel Nightingale (9)
St Veronica's RC Primary School, Rossendale

GOSSIP FOR GIRLS

Gossip for girls is like diamonds, pearls, chocolates
And sweets and much more treats
Always messing with their hair
They hate trying to share
They are always going to parties and
Hate boys who think they're smarties.

Laura-Jane Hindle (8)
St Veronica's RC Primary School, Rossendale

JACK FROST

Watch out! Watch out!
Jack is about
When you're sleeping,
He will be there.
When you're weeping
He's sure to stare.

Watch out! Watch out!
Jack is about
When you're eating,
He will be there.
When you're drinking
He's sure to stare.

Watch out! Watch out!
Jack is about
When you're waking,
He will be there.
When you're aching
He's sure to stare.

Romy Beagan (10)
St Veronica's RC Primary School, Rossendale

WINTER'S DAY

The snow is here, it came today
But doesn't look like it's here to stay
The fluffy white clouds
Have moved away
Let's go inside and get warm
For today.

Aaron Morris (9)
St Veronica's RC Primary School, Rossendale

WHY ARE YOU SO BAD?

If it wasn't you
Who poured de milk on the floor,
Threw de eggs at de wall,
Put yuh mam's ring down the sink,
Painted de kitchen wall pink?

If it wasn't you
Who kicked the cat,
Covered the wall with butter,
Flooded the bathroom,
Messed up your mam's bedroom,
Threw mud balls at your new carpet?
So why do you look so guilty
When you stand in front of mam?

Charlotte Harling (9)
St Veronica's RC Primary School, Rossendale

A TADPOLE TO A FROG

I'm a little tadpole
Look at me
Then strangely some legs appear on me.

I'm a little tadpole
Look at me
Then strangely some arms appear on me.

I'm a little tadpole
Look at me
But not anymore
I'm a frog as you can see.

Clare Burrows (8)
St Veronica's RC Primary School, Rossendale

MY PERFECT ROOM

My room, my room,
My fabulous room,
No toys on the floor,
No scratches on the door,
Pens on my desk,
All looking its best.

Well, this is today when I've put things away
But wait till night my room's a bomb site.

Toys on the floor,
Scratches on the door,
Pens thrown about,
Books left out,
Don't panic, don't lie,
We don't have to cry,
It only takes a while,
When you have a big smile,
To change back the gloom
To my perfect room!

Gerard Manley (9)
St Veronica's RC Primary School, Rossendale

MY CAT RUPERT

My cat Rupert
Is as cheeky as can be
As crafty as a mouse
Just as smart as me!

He lies in front of the fire
Playing with his toys
He stares at the girls
But chases with the boys.

My cat Rupert
When it comes to food,
Munching on his chicken
Sounding very rude.

Finally it's calm
Not a meow not a cry,
Shh be quiet . . .
Rupert says goodbye.

Julianna Brougham (9)
St Veronica's RC Primary School, Rossendale

THE MYSTERIOUS MAN

Sneaky Jack Frost,
Wicked Jack Frost,
Crawling through the grass
On the car,
Down the path,
Where is he now?

Help! Help!
Help me please
He's got my toes
Sparkling white
Grim as night
On the windowpane.

There he is
Up the tree
Chase him up and down
Around the bush
Down the garden
I've got him now.

Jenna Chattwood (9)
St Veronica's RC Primary School, Rossendale

DE PERSON TO BLAME

If it wasn't you
Who tek de butter
And spread on de wall
Splatter de egg
And mek it drip
Jumpy are yu
A puzzel strip to me?

If it wasn't you
Who tek de chalk
And be
Puttin' it on
Me bed now?
Bad is yu
Jumpy are yu
What's de matter with yu?

What's de matter
With yu today
Yu jumpy
Yu lok guilty
Was it yu who did it?

Katherine Parry (8)
St Veronica's RC Primary School, Rossendale

WHY ARE YOU SO SCARED?

If it wasn't you
Who dressed the queen,
Made the cat,
Demolished de bed,
Polished de hat,
Fed the mouse?

If it wasn't you
Who ripped the rug,
Who painted the mut,
Who killed the bug,
Who dropped the bomb
Then why are you so scared?

Jenny Conroy (10)
St Veronica's RC Primary School, Rossendale

CATCH JACK FROST

Jack Frost is here, come and see
His magic has transformed to window
But why? But why? Why is he here,
Last time he froze the garden?

Jack Frost is here, come and see,
He's looking straight at me
Torrential rain is pouring down,
I better sprint inside.

Jack Frost is here come and see
He's sprinkling magic dust
I think I'll run up to my room
And see if I can see him.

Jack Frost is here come and see
He's fading away slightly
Look over there he's disappearing
He'll be back next winter.

Jack Frost is here, come and see
He's fading away in the darkness
I missed my chance to catch him,
But I'll do it next year.

Edward Ainsworth (9)
St Veronica's RC Primary School, Rossendale

JACK FROST

'Watch out! Watch out!'
You're in for a fright,
He is very, very sneaky
I look out the window
And there he is,
He is very cheeky
His eyes are blue
Like the sky
I see him run away
I chase him all over the place
I suddenly lose him
He runs like a mouse
Behind the shed I spot him
Then I lose him again
By taking my eye off him
Beware until next time.

Chelsea Frost (9)
St Veronica's RC Primary School, Rossendale

PARTY TIME

It's party time, it's party time
I open presents up and down
People sing a special song, this is what they sing
'Happy birthday to you,
Happy birthday to you,
Happy birthday to you, you, you, you, you.'
Party hats round with a point on the top
A party cake with a cherry on the top
Chocolate buns with a sprinkle on the top
It's party time, it's party time, yes it is.

Robyn Kay (8)
St Veronica's RC Primary School, Rossendale

OVER DE WALL

If it wasn't you
Who head the ball
Round the corner
Hit de lamp post
Landed on de coast
Was it you?

If it wasn't you
Who kicked de ball
Up in de air
It hit mi hair
I said was it you?

If it wasn't you
Who threw de ball
Over de fence
Down de wall
Smash mi car
I said was it you?

Laura O'Gara (9)
St Veronica's RC Primary School, Rossendale

SNAKES

Snakes, snakes are not nice baked,
Snakes, snakes are sometimes fakes,
Snakes, snakes sometimes live in lakes,
Snakes, snakes sometimes are better than cakes
Snakes, snakes are better than rakes,
Snakes, snakes are better than all the Jakes,
Snakes, snakes are better than gates,
Snakes, snakes are the best ever makes.

Aimee Hilton (8)
St Veronica's RC Primary School, Rossendale

BEWARE TONIGHT!

Beware tonight!
Jack Frost is near
Where you sleep.
Jack Frost is hovering
On the street
On your street.

Beware tonight!
Jack Frost is near
Where you sleep.
Jack Frost is hovering
On the drive
On your drive.

Beware tonight
Jack Frost is near
Where you sleep.
Jack frost is hovering
In the house
In your house.

Charles McIntyre (9)
St Veronica's RC Primary School, Rossendale

BUBBLES

Bubbles floating through the air
Underneath the blue sky's air.
Bubbles wandering around somewhere
Bubbles hiding
Look and find where
Every bubble soon pops
So now there's no more to pop.

Floating in the air so gently
Lightly down to who knows where
Over, round the roofs of houses
Too high to reach
Too low on the ground.

Elizabeth Ainsworth (7)
St Veronica's RC Primary School, Rossendale

CATS SLEEP ANYWHERE

Cats sleep anywhere
On the chair,
On the bear.
Cats sleep anywhere
In a stable,
On a table.
Cats sleep anywhere
In the shop,
On the mop.
Cats sleep anywhere
On a foot,
In some soot.
Cats sleep anywhere
On a book,
On the hook.
Cats sleep anywhere
In a boat,
On a moat.
Cats sleep anywhere,
In a tray,
On the bay.
Cats sleep anywhere.

Daniel Gibirdi (8)
St Veronica's RC Primary School, Rossendale

IF IT WASN'T YUH

If it wasn't yuh who smacked the door
Then how do yuh explain the splinters?
If it wasn't yuh who had a war
Then why do yuh have the bruises.

If it wasn't yuh who kicked the cat
Then why did it start screeching?
If it wasn't yuh who screwed up the mat
Then why is the mat sulking?

If it wasn't yuh who put mud on the floor
Then why is it your footprints?
If it wasn't yuh who kicked the new door
Then why is that door
Screeching?

Catherine Haworth (10)
St Veronica's RC Primary School, Rossendale

SUMMERTIME

At summertime I can see a bright red sun.
At summertime people have fun.
At summertime people go to the beach.
At summertime some schools teach.
At summertime people go to the park.
At summertime people talk.
At summertime people play.
At summertime horses eat hay.
At summertime people get their spades out.
At summertime people do things out and about.
At summertime people read a book.
At summertime people cook.

Adam Cook (8)
St Veronica's RC Primary School, Rossendale

THE JEWEL

In our village
There is a jewel
And it's treasured
By St Veronica's School

It isn't too big
It isn't too small
But the problem is
You have to dig.

You have to dig all day
You have to dig all night
But it all turns out all right
Because they buried it out of sight.

I wish I could find the jewel
But there's a problem because I don't know where it is
Children say it is in a cupboard
Others say the teacher's got it
But what is the point of looking?

Wait a minute, remember the day I said
I saw something in the head teacher's lunch box
Well I am going to risk my life, I am going to get it
Creak, creak oh no I can't do this
One, two, three, ooops the head teacher's going to kill me
Come here now.

Rebecca Slinger (8)
St Veronica's RC Primary School, Rossendale

JACK FROST

Jack Frost is in the garden
I've looked high and low,
He's always here and there,
But he never seems to go.
Jack Frost is in the street,
He's in every puddle
Down every single street,
And he'll get you into trouble.

Jack Frost is in the house
He's all over the place
In every nook and cranny
He thinks he's in a race.
Jack Frost is in the bushes,
He's creeping round and round
You'll see his trail everywhere,
But he'll never make a sound.

Jack Frost is in the greenhouse
He's inside everything
I'm surprised he doesn't make a noise
He never seems to sing.
Jack Frost is everywhere
He's in the air
You never seem to hear him
But he's there, I swear.

William Eaton (9)
St Veronica's RC Primary School, Rossendale

JACK FROST

Jack Frost he is a cheeky boy
With eyes an icy blue
He'll bite your fingers nose and toes
And freeze you all the way through
He'll walk across your garden
And shock everything in sight
I'd never, oh never, oh never go near him
Unless you want frost bite!

Jack Frost he is a sharp little boy
He'll make your nose go red
He'll wake you up in the morning,
But you'll want to stay in bed.
He'll turn your grass into needles
And spider webs into wire.
He'll completely freeze the hottest oven
And cool off the warmest fire!

Jack Frost he is a quick little boy
He's as fast as a racing car!
He'll skid along your drive way
And laugh wickedly 'Ha, ha, ha!'
I've got a cold and a red runny nose
With eyes all dreary and hot.
He's frosty blue and glittering white,
And makes me sneeze a lot!

Lauren Mason (10)
St Veronica's RC Primary School, Rossendale

LIVERPOOL

Fantastic, fabulous Liverpool
They're the best team ever
They can beat Man U and Arsenal
Five - nil at least.
Stupid, silly Everton
They're the worst team ever
Liverpool can beat them easy
It's like playing against some old grannies
When we beat Crystal Palace my favourite goal was . . .
When Fowler got the ball and back heels it to Wanchop
And then Wanchop scored!
Come on you Reds! Come on you Reds!
When the final whistle blew I knew we were in the final
Liverpool are unstoppable,
Liverpool are unbeatable,
Liverpool are best,
Rubbish, useless Man U
They're another rubbish team
They can't even beat Middlesborough
Even though they're top of the league,
They always win by fluke
Messy, sloppy leads
If one of their players go down
He screams like a baby
But none of the Liverpool players do that
Because they're the best team ever.

William Mason (8)
St Veronica's RC Primary School, Rossendale

SCHOOL

School is good,
School is bad,
You have lunch,
You don't have lunch.

In our village
There is a treasure
And that treasure is
Our teacher.

You have a dictionary
Maths,
English,
Computers,
And lots more.

There is lots more work to do
Children come
Children go.

No break for juniors
But a drink of milk for infants,
Coats and coat hangers,
Lots of work,
Lots of play,
There are folders,
There is geography,
There is maths,
And now school is over
Bye!

Natasha Stanley (8)
St Veronica's RC Primary School, Rossendale

JACK FROST

Get out! Get out!
He may be about
He could be painting his picture
He takes the night
And gives you a fright
The sneaky old Jack Frost.

Jack Frost, Jack Frost
Never gets lost
Picking up diamonds and jewels
He's in the house
As sound as a mouse
That sneaky old Jack Frost.

Around the bush,
In the shed,
He'll dance round them
Day and night
And freeze them again
And then disappear
That sneaky old Jack Frost.

Conor McGirr (10)
St Veronica's RC Primary School, Rossendale

MAYBE IT WERE!

If it wasn't you
Then ow was it er?
Well it ain't me
Are yu sure?
It was you weren't it?
Maybe it were.

Well two hours later
We still ain't decided
But I bet it was you
What are we fighting about?

Hannah Valentine (10)
St Veronica's RC Primary School, Rossendale

SCHOOL

I hate school,
I sit on a stool.
Coats hanging,
While chiming,
Leaves dragging,
People hanging.
Computers damaged,
Cabbage damaged,
Food fights,
Plane flights,
White boards,
Skate boards,
Ten tables,
Two neighbours,
Brown trays,
Five days,
Coats and hats,
Brown cats,
Playing games,
Funny games.

Joe Nangle (8)
St Veronica's RC Primary School, Rossendale

SCHOOL

School is good,
School is bad,
School is sometimes
Homework mad.
Coats dragging,
People nabbing,
Children leaving,
It's heaving,
I'm weaving,
While children are leaving,
Hiding in the car,
While mums talk to their pa
But the children screaming
For their ma
I want my mummy
In the car.
Next morning maths first,
Science next
Finished again.

Hannah Connolly (7)
St Veronica's RC Primary School, Rossendale

ALWAYS SHINING

Snow sparkling, glistening, glittering,
Covering everything with its white robe
Sheds like igloos,
Sticks like wands,
Always shining, shining, shining.

Frost sparkling, glistening, glittering,
Covering everything with its silver robe
Leaves like diamonds,
Cobwebs like stars,
Always shining, shining, shining.

Ice sparkling, glistening, glittering,
Covering water with its clear robe
Icicles like spears,
Ponds like ice rinks,
Always shining, shining, shining.

Niamh Baxendale (9)
St Veronica's RC Primary School, Rossendale

SNAILS

You find snails anywhere,
Some in trees,
Some in houses,
Some on chairs,
Some in pairs,
Some on bears,
Some on stairs,
Some in fairs,
Some in fur,
Some in cream,
Some in grass,
Some on roads,
Some have fears,
Some have ears,
Some keep them,
Some love them,
Some don't like them at all,
But they don't care,
Life is sweet,
They're snails.

Thomas Walmsley (8)
St Veronica's RC Primary School, Rossendale

THE HIGHWAYMAN

The moon was a ghostly galleon and the cloud its cloudy sea
The highwayman came on his stallion trotting - trotting - trotting.
The noble highwayman rode - rode - rode
To the old inn where his true love dwells.
He rode into the courtyard tlot - tlot - tlot and tapped - tapped - tapped
On the casement of Bess the landlord's daughter
Oh how he loved the landlord's daughter.
For old Tim the high ostler overheard him saying - saying - saying
He'll bring - bring - bring fine riches back
And return at daybreak or hell might bar the way - way - way
He galloped away - away - away
In the moonlight - moonlight - moonlight.

Then at morn twenty - twenty - twenty of King George's men
Came marching - marching - marching
To the old inn door - door - door
They came and knocked - knocked - knocked they did
They passed through the door to Bess the landlord's daughter
King George's men bound and gagged Bess, the landlord's daughter
They put a musket to her breast
Then a noble highwayman came riding - riding - riding
Down the old lane - lane - lane.
Bess grabbed the trigger - trigger - trigger and fired.

The highwayman in horror flew through the air and died,
For one of the men had killed him
They are now at peace together.

Kristian Garland (9)
Shade Junior & Infant School

116

THE STREET AT NIGHT

Thinking, thinking about the street at night
Thinking, thinking about the fairy light blotted sky,
Yes the one with a hovering orange.
Okay I've decided I'm staying up all night, yes the whole night!
All the time the metronome ticking, frantically.
Most time my eyes flashing, like huge blue blobs
The time seemed to be changing longer, longer.
Outside, starting to sprinkle was cotton wool.
Sometime later now the face was ticking, like a tap dripping,
slowly, slowly.
Soon I crept downstairs, sneakily, sneakily
Next I reached the sheep-rugged pavement and the crystal road
Then suddenly out of nowhere appeared a massive light bulb
It had the strength of one billion candles, approaching rapidly, rapidly
Now slowly, but surely it was becoming morning
Because the birds were singing and fluttering around
Quietly I opened the door and tiptoed back upstairs.
Then, like a cat, I pounced straight into my bed.

Patrick Ramsbottom (9)
Shade Junior & Infant School

THE SUN IS LIKE A CANDLE ILLUMINATING THE WORLD

The sun is a candle illuminating the Earth
Miniature stars are fairies curled up into little balls to escape from harm
The moon is a ghostly galleon spinning in its orbit
Down, down, down below the traffic lights
Are tropical lollipops
Changing from green to red
Stopping when you say '*Bed!*'

Alex Hill (9)
Shade Junior & Infant School

THE HIGHWAYMAN

The road was like a ribbon in the moonlight,
The stars were jewels in the sky.
The moon was a haunted galleon tossed upon the cloudy sea
The highwayman came riding, riding, riding by.

His guns were hanging by his side, waiting to be used,
He had his knife strapped to his thigh-high boots.
It was so quiet not a fox or mouse to be heard,
But then in the distance there was a faint hoot.

When he arrived at the old inn door, guess who he saw?
Bess, the landlord's daughter
The landlord's black-eyed daughter.

But round the corner, behind the shed,
Stood Tim the ostler, his hair like mouldy hay,
Jealous as can be for he loved Bess the landlord's daughter,
The landlord's black-eyed daughter.

Then he heard whispering so as dumb as a dog he listened,
And heard the robber say
I will come back tomorrow only hell should bar the way
He kissed her goodbye and off he rode into the distance.

He didn't come in the evening
He didn't come at noon but St George's men did,
They crept into her bedroom and gagged her on the spot,
They tied her to her bed with a musket at her breast.

Then an idea sprung into mind, she found her finger on the trigger,
Then out of the corner of her eye she saw him
So did St George's men, they were ready, they aimed, they shot him,
Straight in the heart, he fell, Bess had seen all this and shot herself.

The road was like a ribbon in the moonlight,
The stars were jewels in the sky.
The moon was a haunted galleon tossed upon the cloudy sea
The highwayman came riding, riding, riding by.

Elizabeth Uttley (10)
Shade Junior & Infant School

EXCUSES, EXCUSES

'Late again Cullen?'
'Yes Sir.'
'You'll have the cane around your ankles for this.'
'No! I'll tell you why Sir.'
'What is it then?'
'Breakfast Sir, came to life Sir.'
'How?'
'Harry Potter Sir, came to my house Sir, made it come to life Sir.'
'Any others?'
'No Sir.'
'What about yesterday?'
'Elephant Sir. Stuck on the toilet I couldn't go all day Sir.'
'What about afternoon?'
'Elephant blocked the plumbing Sir.'
'Line up for PE.'
'Can't Sir. Don't have my kit Sir.'
'Why not?'
'Sister sir. Went hyper Sir, tore it up Sir.'
'Okay then'.

Ashli Cullen (9)
Shade Junior & Infant School

DREAM

The moon above us was a giant juicy grapefruit
Dancing heel and toe tossed up in the inky black
Were the twinkling stars
Whilst boarding the ropes were snakes clinging to their prey
All cabins had lights on like glowing fairies
Upon the wooden deck we watched the waves jump like dolphins
Against the ship
Little mice were carrying out orders for the captain
Then I crept away down a corridor
Which was a whale's mouth becoming deeper as I ventured
I watched dawn push away dusk and then
Like a phoenix from the flames the sun rose
Night time had turned into
A beautiful bright morning with birds singing
Amazing songs
Flowers blossoming were mouths opening
And to think it was all a dream.

Tamsin Connor (9)
Shade Junior & Infant School

DRAGON

In North Wales no one has lived to tell the tales,
For there is a dragon who can smash a horse and wagon,
And can shake the floor by tapping its claw,
And can fly higher and breathe fire,
Until boiling heat touches his feet,
And energises him until he has got a grin,
And wrestles a giant and he can always win,
So just remember what you have heard,
When the dragon wins, he always grins.

Jack Overall (10)
Shade Junior & Infant School

MILLENNIUM BUG

It's red,
With eyes,
And silver,
With legs.

It crawls,
It spies,
And jumps,
And takes.

But now it's in the computers
And now it's taking over the world
And now it's going to get splattered.

But that's not fair, it was into everything but me!

Trudie Vallender (9)
Shade Junior & Infant School

THE CHRISTMAS NIGHT

In the night, in a house,
Nothing was moving, not even a mouse.

The stars were diamonds very high,
Snow was cotton wool drifting from the sky.

Boys and girls asleep in their beds,
Wrapped up in blankets, resting their heads.

The moon was as bright as glowing cat's eyes,
Christmas stockings were delicious mince pies.

Was there a rumble in the house?
Was it Santa or was it a mouse?

Lucy Greenwood (10)
Shade Junior & Infant School

SUMMER

Sparkling water trickling over waterfalls,
Beautiful landscapes to walk over,
Plenty of wildlife around,
The world is more beautiful this time of year,
Blue skies where the sun shines,
Make new friends on holidays,
Playing out after tea, playing team games,
Beautiful red skies at night,
Not knowing the adventures you're going to have,
New life in the garden,
Long bike rides along the canal,
The water sparkling alongside,
Fresh water from the river,
Just ripe fruit from the garden, very tasteful,
Climbing trees, sparkling hair,
Great big smiles on everybody's face,
Summer's great!

Elizabeth Stansfield (9)
Shade Junior & Infant School

I WANT IT NOW!

Eggs in my basket
Colourful and yummy
I want the biggest egg
I want it in my tummy.

I've got little ones
Medium eggs as well
I want the egg
Give it to me or I'll tell.

I need it right now
I need the biggest egg
So she gave me the egg
I don't want this, I want the smallest egg I said.

Heather Fairbridge (10)
Shade Junior & Infant School

WINTER

Snow, cotton wool falling softly
Shouting children charging down the street
Snowball fights in the park
Children sledging down the flattened hill
Then it reaches us, the time we all enjoy
The lights on the tree are glittering fairies
Next day is time for presents
Which is children's delight
That's winter!

Christopher Wrench (10)
Shade Junior & Infant School

TEN SECONDS BEFORE NEW YEAR

New Year's Day is the same as a newly hatched chick
The excitement grows as a raging fire through dry grass
The seconds pass like hours
But the clock still ticks the very same time
And then there are the last ten seconds before you shout
Hip, hip, hooray
For the midnight brings the New Year cheer!

James Kidd (9)
Shade Junior & Infant School

How Scary Is The Wind?

Wind at night on your window like a ghost
Screaming, banging on your windowpane.

You tell your friends that you're not scared
But really you are inside when you're in your bed
The ghost comes, trying to get in.

The ghost comes shaking the trees
So that all the ghosts awake
So sleep tight!

Emily Harrop (10)
Shade Junior & Infant School

Space

The stars are jewels dancing heel to toe
The sun is a huge hot basketball floating in the sky
The face of the moon is a never-ending smile
Seven planets are multicoloured footballs stuck in mid-air
And the clouds are spilt blobs of paint.

Robert Carlton (9)
Shade Junior & Infant School

Ghana

There was a man from Ghana
Who insisted on playing on the piano
One day his hand slipped
His head flipped and out popped
A biting piranha.

Leoni Johnson (11)
Water County Primary School

PUSSY

All is quiet,
Nothing but the gentle purring sound of pussy stretched out on the mat,
She's dreaming of a far away land,
But there's still one thing awake,
Her tail.
Maybe it's a sword,
Fighting an evil demon,
Or a snake,
Slithering along.
Whatever it is it looks magical,
Swaying from side to side.
But all is quiet,
Nothing but the gentle purring sound of pussy stretched out on the mat.

Alex Maxwell (10)
Water County Primary School

TOBY

Toby, Toby with his coat golden brown,
His tail shone like a moonlit crown.
All of his mane was so tender and fine,
He looked like a statue made out of pine.
The children stared at the magnificent sight,
And couldn't sleep all through the night.
For they dreamt of my horse with blue crystal eyes,
Whom upon the floor at night he lies.

Anthony Smith (11)
Water County Primary School

THE FARMER

As he walked up the hill towards the sky
He began to round up his sheep with his dog named Fly
Fly was quick,
Fly was fast,
But Meg was passed in a blast.

The sheep were jumping
Meg's heart was pumping
Along with Fly it was like a race
But together they worked fine as a brace.

He heard a noise whilst in the meada
It was his son
On the muckspreada.

The farmer works in snow and hail
In wind and rain he will prevail
Delivering his milk he will never fail
Even though his Lannie is as slow as a snail.

This may sound like trouble and strife
But this is the farmer's way of life.

Stephen Cashinella (11)
Water County Primary School

CAR JOURNEY

Are we nearly there?
Are we nearly there?
This journey is taking ever so long
And no one seems to care.

Are we nearly there?
Are we nearly there?
Somewhere there should be a turning
But we haven't got a clue where.

Are we nearly there?
Are we nearly there?
I think that Dad has got us lost
Because he is growling like a bear.

Are we nearly there?
Are we nearly there?
I could be sat back at home
In a comfy chair!

Are we nearly there?
Are we nearly there?
At last we have finally found it
We are going to the fair!

Chantelle Noon (11)
Water County Primary School

My Magic Kite

I have a new kite,
It goes such a height,
It took me on a flight,
It lasted all night,
I saw trees as big as my knees,
An elephant's ear stretch along a pier,
I saw a big deer.

I wonder what happened next?

Matthew Guest (10)
Water County Primary School

My Mum

My mum is sometimes nice
But the problem is she's scared of mice.
My mum loves dogs
But she doesn't like frogs.
My mum is naughty
Because she hates to party.
My mum sometimes gets upset
So I buy her a pet.

Racheal Jordan (10)
Water County Primary School

MY KITE

I have a kite
It goes such a height
All by myself I tied the string
But the next day it just went *ping!*
Up into the sky it went
I think it landed over in Kent
So I asked my dad to go and get it
My dad replied 'You can forget it.'
So I saved up my money
And!
I have a new kite
It goes such a height.

Jack Roderick (11)
Water County Primary School

CAR SICK

'Are we there yet?'
'Are we there yet?'
'Just another minute Daddy's little pet.'
'You said that ages ago and I need a wee.'
'Be quiet and I will buy you McDonald's for tea.'
'Dad, Dad, Dad I am going to be . . . oops, sorry Dad.'
'Now I have a bucket and a sponge guess what I have to do?'

Natalie Hardstaff (11)
Water County Primary School

HEADMASTER FROM HELL

I walked into the classroom
It was full of doom and gloom.
At the front was a six-foot hairy thing
With a beard that looked like bits of string.
The eyes burned a deep blood red,
Oh God I thought I'd soon be dead.
It had a large and bulbous nose,
The shoes could hardly contain its toes.
Its large and protruding belly,
Proved to me it watched too much telly.
It said, 'Come in and take a seat,
I think you're in for a treat.'
'Err . . . err . . . it's all right' I stutter.
'I'd better go, you look like a nutter.'
I fled out into the yard,
I was off I was on my guard.
All of a sudden out he came,
Hardly looking very tame.
Gasping and glaring he looked insane,
No way will I ever go there again.

Reece Taylor (10)
Water County Primary School